T0194343

At Worship's Core

Core Values
for the
Contemporary
Worship Leader

TOM MCDONALD, PHD

WESTBOW
PRESS®
A DIVISION OF THOMAS NELSON
& ZONDERVAN

WestBow Press books may be ordered through booksellers or by contacting:

WestBow Press
A Division of Thomas Nelson & Zondervan
1663 Liberty Drive
Bloomington, IN 47403
www.westbowpress.com
1 (866) 928-1240

All Scriptures, unless otherwise noted, are taken from the New Life Version (NLV). Copyright © 1969, 2003 by Christian Literature International. Used by permission. All rights reserved.

Scripture quotations marked KJV are taken from the King James Version of the Bible.

Scripture quotations marked NKJV are taken from the New King James Version®. Copyright © 1982 by Thomas Nelson. Used by permission. All rights reserved.

ISBN: 978-1-9736-6337-9 (sc)
ISBN: 978-1-9736-6338-6 (hc)
ISBN: 978-1-9736-6339-3 (e)

Library of Congress Control Number: 2019906571

Print information available on the last page.

WestBow Press rev. date: 7/31/2019

For Denise …

Always caring

Always charming

Always elegant

Praise for "A Worship's Core"

This significant work by worship leader, professor, and author, Dr. Tom McDonald, immediately captured my attention! The title itself, *At Worship's Core*, stirred my heart, and I was drawn into the riches of its contents. With wisdom that comes from over twenty-five years of ministry experience in leading congregations in worship as well as the evident hand of the Lord at work in Tom's life, this book is worthy of the highest accolades. I am enriched and impacted. A profound statement from its pages reveals the purity, motivation, and character of its author. His prayer is, "Lord, what can I sing just for You? What do the people need from Your hand, Lord?" I have been challenged, as a result, to a deeper reverence and a more joyful, authentic worship.

—Glenn C. Burris Jr., President, The Foursquare Church

Dr. Tom McDonald has succeeded in his attempt to reveal what is and how a worship leader should be. His passion to raise a new generation of worship leaders can be seen in this book. He has revealed the secrets of the texture and the nature of worship, which will enable the worship leaders to prepare and lead the congregation into the presence of God and respond. His immense wisdom and experience being a worship leader equips him to speak aloud on this subject. The book will be an eye-opener to all who want to worship God in spirit and truth.

—Pastor Daniel Kizhakkevila, Chief Pastor of Full Gospel Churches in India, President of Voice of Gospel Ministries International

On the first day of Hebrew school in medieval Europe, children would sometimes undergo the ritual of kissing honey from the Torah. Sometimes the honey would be kissed off a slate with the letters of the Hebrew alphabet. That's twenty-two kisses. Tom McDonald has written, not a five-star book, but a twenty-two-kiss book. The sweet spirit of worship fills every page and chapter. The word we translate as "worship" literally means to "kiss toward," and this book is a textbook in how worship can be a holy kiss back toward the God who kissed us into life and keeps us alive, kiss by kiss.

—Leonard Sweet, author of *The Bad Habits of Jesus*, professor, and founder of www.preachthestory.com

In the formative years of my ministry journey, I had the unique privilege of being impacted by the teaching and life of Tom McDonald. A teacher, a mentor, and an example, Tom was and is all of these things. His heart has tasted the beauty and scope of God's Kingdom, which of course, is infused with constant worship. This book is an alabaster box, broken open on the feet of Jesus's body, for us to receive a fresh anointing and hunger for the presence and glory of our King. If you truly wish to experience the beauty of worship that is transformational, this book will be a faithful guide."

—Dr. Robert Stearns, Eagles Wings Founder, Bishop of The Tabernacle, Orchard Park, New York

Coupled with education and experience, Tom McDonald shares his purpose and passion that is pitch-perfect! Balancing scripture and song, he offers step-by-step insights to assist in understanding the "worth-ship" of the triune God. Both life and leadership will be renewed and revitalized by Dr. McDonald's poignant words encouraging personal prayer, planning, and preparation for private and public praise.

—Mark Thallander, former organist at The Crystal Cathedral, President of the Mark Thallander Foundation

ACKNOWLEDGMENTS

Any author will agree that a book is a labor of love that includes the advice of many devoted individuals. Mine is no exception. To begin, I acknowledge two men who felt my work in the professoriate was worthy of print.

Thank you, Mohanan Unni, my former doctoral student, and Samuel Varghese, an Indian venture capitalist, for your belief in me and generous underwriting of my manuscript. I am indebted to my pastors for their theological insight. They include Jack W. Hayford, Earl D. Baldwin, and Jim Tolle. Gentlemen, you were faithful. Well done!

I was blessed beyond measure by the musical instruction of my three conducting professors, the inimitable Saul Lilienstein, my mentor Vincent P. Lawrence, and, of course, Peabody's own Edward Polochick.

Editorial support came from the wise and prophetic Marilyn Price, my gifted sister-in-law Beth McDonald, and the peerless staff of editors at Westbow Press..

Further support came from my loving family—Denise, my incomparably lovely wife, and our incredible sons, Michael, Christian, and Gabriel. Finally, to the two choirs, I was privileged to conduct for decades, who loved me through thick and thin and taught me so much about the dynamism of the rehearsal process. I love you back and always will!

CONTENTS

FOREWORD

It is an honor to lift my pen today to ascribe a fitting introduction for my colleague and friend, Dr. Tom McDonald. Tom and I share a passion for the purpose of worship. For nearly a decade he administered our Department of Music at The Church On The Way in Los Angeles. During those wonderful days, he oversaw the growth and development of a robust ministry with choirs and worship teams, bands, orchestras, and world-class rhythm sections. What is more, I would be remiss not to mention the contingent of professional studio performers who attended our church, by virtue of our proximity to Hollywood, and their love and esteem for Tom.

I am being intentional in detailing the depth of his ministry portfolio because Tom's multifaceted gifts for leadership are essential to understanding the value of this manuscript. He is, you see, not only a talented musician but one who possesses a rare kind of pastor's heart. It was his heart for the things of God that first caught my attention in what, I must confess, was nothing short of a divine appointment. The year was 1993. Tom was chosen to lead worship at the same conference that I was guest speaker. This event on *Worship in the Church* was conducted by the Assemblies of God Theological Seminary. On the second evening of our gathering, I was invited to a green room event before my preaching assignment. As I walked down the long corridor next to the auditorium, my aide and I noticed two identical doors on the left. We chose the second door.

To my surprise, we entered a rather unadorned broom closet in which Dr. McDonald had gathered the worship team before the evening service. Immediately I was taken by his spiritual discernment with regard for what was about to happen. He was actually ministering grace to those musicians when I would have expected a musical pep talk. I chose to stay, fully cognizant of the fact that I was in the wrong room. Or was I?

As Tom led the students in a time of devotion and surrender, I joined in his godly pursuit. Worship is the invitation for Jesus to enter any congregation—bringing peace, pardon, and perspective. It is as if our Lord is standing behind a curtain and the singing is His cue! But none of that can occur if the worship leader or the team is out of sorts with the Lord. Tom intuitively understands that component of leadership mentality. As I watched him function—not as a musician but as pastor—I felt the hand of God calling me to invite him, subsequently, to come to Southern California and partner with us. Clearly what appeared to be the wrong door was, in fact, the right door!

Finally I am taken by Tom's potent title, *At Worship's Core.* At the center of worship, administration is a core value summoning musicians and pastors to bow the knee and inquire of the Lord just what He might want us to sing and say each time the body gathers for a worship encounter. This book reminds us that effective leading worship is about "renewing our strength" before planning the worship repertoire (Isaiah 40:31). In fact, one should wait on the Lord prior to any ministerial endeavor.

And for that concept alone, I tip my hat!

Jack W. Hayford, Pastor Emeritus
The Church On The Way

PREFACE

Shortly after World War II in the ashy morning light of Leningrad, a Russian guard spotted an elderly man walking amid the rubble with a cane and war-torn overcoat. The area in question was restricted. As such, the guard spoke sharply, "Halt! Who are you? Where are you going?"

The gentleman, caught unaware, was startled. Approaching the soldier slowly, he paused and cleared his voice. "What was that you said, Officer?"

"You heard me," he snapped. "Who are you? Where are you going?"

The old man, a wise rabbi, responded, "Actually, Officer, I have a question for you! How much does the Russian government pay you a month to guard this neighborhood? Whatever it is, I'll double your pay if you'll simply follow me around and ask me those two questions every day for the rest of my life: *Who are you? Where are you going?*"

The message of this story is timeless. It is easy for us to lose ourselves in the hard times of ministry life. When stress builds, unexpected disappointments mount, and the harshness of working with difficult or irregular people proliferates, it is easy to mislay our core values. What's more, when fads or trends seek to redefine us, we may miss the mark if we do not know who God made us to be. In those precarious moments, we may find ourselves struggling to hear the "still, small voice of God."

Walking about in the aftermath of a cataclysm, the rabbi, trying to find purpose in trauma, immediately saw the wisdom in applying the soldier's questions to his daily life. In uncertain times, dear reader, knowing the ingredients *At Worship's Core* are essential to thriving on the other side of conflict, chaos, and disillusionment. I have been there more than once. And I attest to the aforementioned statements.

I will build this preface then on the outline the austere Russian soldier presented to the nameless rabbi so long ago.

Who Are You?

I'm a veteran worship leader who was fortunate enough to serve two wonderful congregations over a thirty-five-year arc of time. I did so amid the Jesus Revolution and the Charismatic Renewal. I witnessed the reformation of church worship, the establishment of contemporary Christian music, and the proliferation of mega-churches all across the United States. Moreover, I was invited to serve what Christian sociologists refer to as "one of the ten most innovative churches in America."

Jack W. Hayford pastored The Church On The Way for over thirty years. Toward the end of his pastorate, *Christianity Today* featured him on the cover of their magazine with the tagline "The Pentecostal Gold Standard." His influence was global; his understandings about worship transformed me.

It was Pastor Jack who told me the story of the founder of the Foursquare denomination, Aimee Semple McPherson, who had emblazoned on her pulpit the phrase, "We would see Jesus." His overarching legacy to me was just that: the singing in worship is all about Jesus, welcoming Him and waiting on Him as well as magnifying Him and worshipping Him. By grace, I stood right next to him while he modeled that principle for nearly a decade.

Besides that, I am also a fifth-generation teacher.

My ancestry courageously taught both Native Americans in teepees as well as participated after school in the Underground Railroad during the Civil War era. These were women of fortitude and commitment who knew that education was a pathway out of poverty and repression. They valued the human spirit. They tried to make their world a better place. Their blood is my blood. Their heart is my heart. And their passion for a classroom was passed down through my own grandmother, a high school English teacher in the Depression, and my mother, an elementary reading scholar. As such, I inherently understand a classroom.

In addition to my service in the pastorate, I spent twenty-five years in the professoriate teaching worship leaders, pastors, and lay leaders to grasp the subtleties of "coming into His presence with singing" (see Psalm 100:1–2).

When recently approached by East Indian venture capitalists and asked to transfer my college lecture notes into a book or two, I was humbled. At this stage of my life and ministry, I saw this opportunity as a mission, a blessing, and a privilege.

So, I have triangulated this invitation to write this text to three cohorts of Christ- followers, namely

- **Worship leaders** associated with the Middle Eastern church movement, my beloved colleagues, who do their very best to entreat the presence of Christ each time they gather
- **Contemporary worship leaders** in the United States for whom much has been given and for whom we, of my generation, contend for the expansion of their borders
- **Pastors**—regardless of denominational stripe—with regard to leading and loving the gift of the worship leader on their staff

Each time you read the term *church*, please know that I am referring at once to the Indian house church and the American local church.

In short, dear reader, I am a minister with godly influences and a gracious heritage.

Where Are You Going?

I believe unpacking this book's title answers the question of where I am going. This is a book about core values. *At Worship's Core* is a carefully examined investigation of the attitudes and behaviors that welcome the presence of the Lord in a church sanctuary or church environment. Leading worship well appears easy, but its effectiveness over time is wrapped in nuance and complexity. Many believe worship is exclusively a musical proposition. And while the vast propensity of worship in church involves singing, I propose that worship is not about the voice but the heart.

Worship, at its core, is the process by which we develop a devotional stance before Almighty God—as we sing, pray, and grow more attentive to His Word and will. Creating that mystical moment in church presupposes a myriad of activity that scaffolds listening skills over musical abilities. Indeed, hearing from the Lord informs the choices a worship leader makes with regard to the song material employed on a Sunday. Hearing from the Lord also enhances the worship leader's ability to negotiate the inevitable personality conflicts that occur behind the scenes of any organization. Finally, hearing from the Lord sensitizes a worship leader to consider songs that, when anointed in public gatherings, give grace in hardship and peace amid the unforeseen storm. Only the Holy Spirit can guide us—you and me—to consider that kind of song ahead of time when we do not know the nature of an individual congregant's personal need.

Beyond a description of the title of my book, I'd also like to underscore the intent of the subtitle, *Core Values for the Contemporary Worship Leader.* Many will assume that the use of the word *contemporary* portends a book about musical style, that is, rhythm sections replacing choirs. But I would caution restraint. My understanding of the term in light of this book's subtitle suggests that being contemporary—or current—affects every aspect of a well-rounded worship leader's job description. For example:

- A contemporary worship leader is one who remains on the cutting edge of technology, lifelong learning and personal disciplines,
- A contemporary worship leader is available to receive daily manna from the Lord regardless of the schedule, the advent of creativity or one's personal fatigue,
- A contemporary worship leader is not only a worthy servant and benevolent boss, but a committed parent and supportive spouse,
- A contemporary worship leader is becoming a master musician— continuing to study, to practice and to model excellence (as a vocalist or instrumentalist) for the next generation,
- A contemporary worship leader is ever present—in real time— pastoring his/her flock by means of intercession, mentorship and fellowship,
- A contemporary worship leader is relentless in the removal of any clog in the phone line to heaven when planning the flow of worship for the next rehearsal, service or special event.

This treatise will encapsulate all of these values and more. I'm excited! So with cane and tattered overcoat, let's delve in.

Tom McDonald, PhD
Los Angeles, CA

Worship is our glad response for the immense grace of our triune God.

—Marva Dawn

INTRODUCTION

One of my interests as a communicator is noting the many times the number three appears in life, art, and theology. In baseball, for example, three strikes and you're out. In the movies, we all recall the Three Stooges, the Three Musketeers, and the Three Amigos. In debate parlance, there is the strategy of thesis, antithesis, and synthesis.

Personally speaking, my grandfather, my father, and I each had three sons! Functionally speaking, a stool has three legs, and so does a photographer's tripod. Grammatically speaking, a strong conclusion sentence often has three clauses. A musicologist will listen to two pieces by a composer and offer a comparison, but after listening to three compositions, one begins to offer contrasts. The former is about similarities, but the latter, with deepening perception, is about appreciating differences.

In the Bible one also notes what some commentators have observed that "three days, in symbolic language, points to an act of divine intervention."[1] Jonah was in the belly of the fish for three days. Paul was blinded on the road to Damascus for three days. Our Lord Jesus was in the grave for three days!

What's more, there are:

- Three theological virtues: faith, hope, and love (1 Corinthians 13)
- Three attributes of God, the One who is Gracious, Compassionate, and Merciful (Exodus 33:18–19).
- Three patriarchs: Abraham, Isaac, and Jacob

---

[1] "The Symbolic Significance of the Third Day In Scripture," http://www.agapebiblestudy.com/documents/The%20Symbolic%20Significance%20of%20the%20third%20day.htm.

Most importantly, we acknowledge the Three in One: Father, Son, and Holy Spirit.

Father God is omniscient (Genesis 21:33), omnipotent (Revelation 19:6), and omnipresent (Ezekiel 48:35). Our Lord Jesus is the way, the truth, and the life (John 14:6). The precious Holy Spirit comforts, guides, and enlightens (John 6:7; Romans 8:14; John 16:13).

As a matter of fact, most worship services juxtapose three components: the Congregational Worship, the Pastoral Teaching, and the Holy Communion, or Altar Service.

In the private life of a public worship leader, the necessity of a three-strand cord cannot be overlooked.

> *Truly the number three is meaningful to God.*

Scripture states, "A threefold cord is not quickly broken" (Ecclesiastes 4:12 KJV). This verse speaks to me of the necessity of a support system the pastoral musician must develop early on with his or her spouse and the Lord so there is a purposeful communion in times of plenty or famine. You see, it is in this very intimate relationship that a worship leader finds sustenance, direction, and prophetic insight.

However, even before one gets married, I believe God is at work building a leader. His process of bolstering a leader prior to anointing the leader is fascinating. God's ways are far above ours. We tend to think of a worship leader's pathway into Christian service from the perspective of music education and charisma. A young, gifted student will polish an inherent talent for songwriting by studying composition or poetry, will keep fit by using a gym, or will gig around town until one's nerves—being in public—are accommodated by sheer grit and determination. But those considerations are only part of the process.

Beyond what we can see from a musical perspective about a young person with talent are the extraordinary purposes of heaven. God often places the desires in the heart of young, potential worship leaders to consider Him early in life. He did so with me. Looking back, it is obvious to me that He lovingly created opportunities for me to be at the right place and right time to learn of Him in others I admired, to think about my destiny at the hands of pastors, authors, and peers from whom I gained insight and perspective, and, more importantly, to begin for myself to reverence the "still, small voice of God" so often ignored in our culture. When Jesus said to Peter, "Upon this rock, I will build my church" (Matthew 16:18), He was inferring that the building of a ministry is a tandem effort between heaven and earth, between the Lord and the worship leader.

In matters of ministry, we are all dependent upon the Lord. "Seek first the Kingdom of God and His righteousness, and all these things shall be added to you" (Matthew 6:33 NKJV). Why is this so? It may be so because worship has become an incendiary term. Worship has the capacity to coalesce a congregation to accomplish great acts of faith. If mishandled though, worship can confuse and cause strife within the church. Simply mentioning the term brings to the surface a confluence of complex feelings. Today's worship leader must carefully lead congregants out of the morass of their private lives and into God's presence where the problems of our lives diminish as we perceive His matchless love, concern, care, and unlimited grace.

Worship is at once personal and public. Curiously, it is in public that we often gain insight into our private challenges and choices. I see the singing process in church as a backstage pass, a green light, or a pathway into the presence of the Lord. This green light is for "whosoever will" (Revelation 22:17). Many American congregants do not ever receive the pass, much less be accepted on the pathway. Before we can actualize a theology of worship, we must, I feel, address the elephant in the "sanctuary."

Worship has many facets. In my country, corporate worship has become somewhat divisive. Certain facets of the worship process are cleaned and dusted regularly. Therefore, they glow! Still other facets are ignored, left dirty and dusty. This need not be. In the book of John, we find the story of Jesus speaking to Peter. This legendary conversation takes place in John 21:15–19.

> Jesus said to Simon Peter, "Do you love Me more than these?"
>
> "Yes, Lord," he said, "You know that I love You."
>
> Jesus said, "Feed My lambs."

Again Jesus said, "Simon, son of John, do you love Me?"

He answered, "Yes, Lord, You know that I love You."

Jesus said, "Take care of My sheep."

The third time Jesus said to Peter, "Do you love Me?"

Peter felt bad because Jesus asked him the third time.

"Do you love Me?"

He said, "Lord, You know everything. You know I love You."

Jesus said, "Feed My sheep.

I tell you, when you were young you put on your belt and went wherever you wanted to go. When you get old you will put out your hands and someone else will put on your belt and take you away where you do not want to go" (indicating his death).

Then Jesus said, "Follow Me."

The implication of this passage is noteworthy. Notice that in asking Peter if he loved Jesus multiple times, our Lord used different terms to identify the ages of the sheep. Jesus spoke of lambs and sheep, younger and older animals, in the same flock.

The application of this lesson is clear. Worship leaders have a primal responsibility to address the felt needs of all the members of the congregation during a worship encounter. Older lambs have different needs than younger ones.

This passage of scripture is self-evident. Jesus loves everyone regardless of age. So should we as worship leaders by choosing repertoire that is meaningful to all.

A Generational Perspective on Worship

Those who have historic traditions view the worship encounter through horn-rimmed glasses, so popular in a different era. Others who are new to faith simply want to make joyful sounds! Amid that kind of diversity one thing is clear: worship becomes volatile if not properly administered. By managing a music ministry haphazardly, one easily forgets the sheer power an eclectic worship repertoire holds for all—regardless of age—who simply want to draw close to God. It is shortsighted to sing only the songs of the worship leader's personal preference or of his or her generation. Yet so many do.

Put simply, because of medical advances, most congregations in the States now have four generations present on any given Sunday. Each generation holds a particular repertoire as sacred. This rock-solid sociological fact puts worship leaders in a predicament.

When the style of a song becomes the paramount issue, not our willingness to welcome His presence, the portion of the congregation who are ignored grow apathetic. Grace lifts, and people leave the way they entered. Perhaps that is why one of my mentors taught me, "God is waiting 'in the wings,' and worship is the invitation to which He responds." The variable in this equation is the term *worship*. For congregational singing to be authentic, capable of reaching past the roof of the church and into the heavenlies, the singing must be participative, unified, and its repertoire not only generationally inclusive but commonly understood.

In fact, songs are memorials we build to celebrate (remember) the acts of Jesus in our lives. When you think about it, certain songs naturally become altars. For example, if one came to faith in Jesus fifty years ago, hymns and gospel songs were the norm. That was the essential worship repertoire commonly sung in those days.

> *Worship becomes holy when all present are invited to serve, to magnify the King, and to minister to the Lord. Then and only then do the songs move the hand of God.*

My mother found faith sitting with her two towheaded little boys watching a black-and-white television one evening in the living room of our family home. We were watching a Billy Graham crusade. After the evangelist spoke, a large choir sang the hymn, "Just as I Am."

I was mesmerized! I too discovered not only faith but a call to ministry. So you can understand my passion for a fully robed music ministry. Singing a hymn today reminds us of God's faithfulness long ago and thereby inspires worship for that cohort of believers.

By the same token, if believers came to the Lord in the last five years, they may just fall in love with guitar-driven worship. Consider these two propositions: People attach preference to experience. People basically resist change.

Most mature believers retain a preference for the music that was being sung during the big events of their lives. Music triggers memory. To complicate this issue, the style or genre used in church today has radically changed. Do you sense a disconnection yet?

Older congregants rarely receive the gift of memory when they sing in church today. Younger congregants frequently miss the opportunity of making memories with the classic hymns of the church. Worship, in that regard, is a double-edged sword. Persons now tend to choose a house of worship based on their music preferences rather than on family tradition or spiritual leading. If I have one singular regret looking back over my decades of service, it is an observation that poor leadership choices were made in changing the look and sound of the chancel.

In short, we did not explain very well why we were making the worship changes. We fired a lot of capable church musicians and used contemporary worship to serve some arbitrary need to stay relevant rather than to glorify the Lord and welcome His presence. Arguably, in the process, we have diminished the value of song in the worship context.

Make no mistake. I have nothing against new songs or contemporary worship. As a matter of fact, I play and sing the repertoire all the time. Frankly, my concern is pastoral, not musical. I care about people. I hunger for all who attend a worship service to sense His manifest presence. Unfortunately, when people are disenfranchised from their traditions without coaching or proper information, they become wounded, frustrated, and embittered. Process dominates content, and style can trump substance. Then the body wains.

Neither a choral hymn tune nor a guitar-driven worship chorus is inherently good or bad, right or wrong. It's just that we in the American church have focused too often on style. Style should subordinate to substance. By making style the focus, congregations focus on the sound rather than the Savior.

To be aware of the pitfalls and dangers of a worship war is to guard against letting such needless church conflict proliferate in your community.

> *Worship is sacramental, not programmatic.*

Above the entrance of the American Library of Congress are etched these words, "Knowledge is Power." Truly that phrase is applicable to this dialogue. In this instance, to know is to be forewarned. Beware, dear friend, lest the besetting sin of youthful arrogance befall your church.

Worship was meant for all God's children, not for a specific generation or some convoluted church growth theory.

In this book:

- I want to convey my passion for the scriptures as they relate to the depth of a song's value. When we sing, wonderful things can happen just beyond the gaze of the human eye.
- I want to communicate how vital the worship encounter is in God's plan to restore and rejuvenate. Worship is strategic to humanity's welfare. We find strength when we sing the song of the Lord in unity and vitality.
- Finally I want to share lessons learned along the way with my readers, in regions where I haven't yet had the privilege to visit, so they can grow and be nurtured in their faith, leadership, and musicianship.

To serve the Lord—as fully formed worship leaders—is to understand the

> *To serve is to sing!*

basic construct of scripture, "Come before His Presence with singing!" (Psalm 100:2 NKJV). Singing soothes. Singing reframes our perspective and massages grace into the troublesome issues we face. Singing brings the Lord close. Therefore, I encourage you to join me, as together we pray, "Open my eyes so that [we] may see wondrous things in Your law" (Psalm 119:18 NKJV). In brief, a worship leader has a sacred trust to sing the songs that all in the church remember.

I have had the great honor of leading Christian worship for decades. In that time, I've developed a deep respect for what a song can do in the life of a congregation, a family, or an individual Christ follower. To be invited then in this new stage of my life to write a book from the perspective of the lessons I have learned at worship's core is amazingly gratifying and deeply humbling.

Perhaps the eminent theologian, Eugene Peterson, could aid us here with his definition of a philosophy of worship. "Worship is the strategy by which we interrupt our preoccupation with ourselves and attend to the Presence of God." Much of my book will unpack his terms *interrupt* and *attend*. For now, however, let us soak in his priceless insight and discern how a theology of worship differs from a practical philosophy of worship ministry.

"Now bring me a musician."
Then it happened, when the musician played, that
the hand of the LORD came upon him.

—2 Kings 3:15

Put it this way: if your idea of God, if your idea of the salvation offered in Christ, is vague or remote, your idea of worship will be fuzzy and ill-formed. The closer you get to the truth, the clearer becomes the beauty, and the more you will find worship welling up within you. That's why theology and worship belong together. The one isn't just a head trip; the other isn't just emotion.

—N. T. Wright[2]

[2] "20 Inspiring Quotes about Worship," http://www.mediashout.com/inspiring-worship-quotes.

CHAPTER 1

AT THE CORE: PART 1

A theology of worship differs from a philosophy of ministry in this way: a theology is a study of what God has said; a philosophy is a blueprint of how to accomplish what God said through Christian service. Perhaps the baseline of worship theology is found in John 4:24 (NKJV), "God is Spirit and those who worship Him must worship in spirit and truth."

"God Is Spirit"

Father God does not possess a physical body. He has always existed. He is everywhere at the same time. These qualities boggle the mind and suggest something important. To worship Him in spirit means, quite literally, we activate this process from our core. "From deep within," the faithful sing.

That kind of devotion informs the quality of the concentration, the openness of heart, and a thoughtful, childlike innocence as we worship God. In other words, the more teachable we are, the deeper the quality of our participation. Congregational singing is, after all, about being obedient to worshipping Him in spirit and in truth. Now there is rich treasure to mine here.

God often communicates with His children through impulse and impression—spirit to spirit. We can access His wisdom, direction, healing, and will as we sing. However, our singing must be accompanied with joy, ease, and delight. If duty or obligation motivates our response, we fall short. Spirit-to-spirit singing occurs when the faithful understand the multifaceted nature of this divine activity.

Over years of ministry, I have gained a profound reverence for activity conducted in sanctuary space, for it is there—among the people—that I have been repurposed. To the naked eye, singing in church is a matter of protocol, tradition, or ritual. But worshipping in spirit is quite a different matter indeed. Understanding this nuance is critical.

The fact of the matter is that singing in spirit transforms a sanctuary into an emergency room. Activity abounds. Souls are revived. Burdens are lifted. Beloved, lives are delivered and changed as we sing from the heart!

"Those Who Worship Him"

Think of the term *worship* as "worthship." To authentically worship God is to give Him His due, to honor Him solely because He is worthy. Worship is the act of bestowing rectitude on the Creator. He is the One who does all things well. He is just, compassionate, and loving. Moreover, He is good. He is faithful to a thousand generations (Deuteronomy 7:9). Whatever we worship, we imitate.

To worship Jehovah, God Almighty, is to take on His character and characteristics. In short, songs provide an escalator into the spirit realm where the business of the Kingdom occurs. This includes the forgiving of sins, the healing of memory, the restoring of relationships, the impartation of wisdom, and the empowering of the fruits and gifts of the Spirit. When we worship, we are restored, renewed, and redeemed. We are cleansed by the Spirit and the Word of the muck of the past.

"Must Worship in Spirit and Truth"

To worship in spirit is not exclusively about the quality of our voice, the energy of our body language, or even an attitude of respect and reverence while in the house. Rather it is about worshipping Jesus from the very thing that is unique about us, our heart. To sing from our hearts is to get lost in His presence with no hint of concern about what others might think. Singing from the heart is a sacred act. In that reverential moment, we are awestruck. We somehow connect our adoration with the praise and worship occurring in heaven itself.

At worship's core, the posture of our heart matters, for out of a believer's heart flows our devotion, our veneration, and our love. My remarks defining and applying John 4:24 are offered to inform the way in which fruitful worship leaders live, for the life of the worship leader provides the kind of atmosphere whereby the saints can grow and develop. The worship leader's life exhibits a set of impeccably high personal and professional guidelines.

Worship is holy, and those who lead worship must "be holy as God is holy" (Leviticus 19:2). Worship leaders must live above reproach. Reproach is a term used to describe the opposite of living in a realm of proper conduct and decorum. One might say of a leader who maintains decorum in all things is that he or she has an excellent spirit, or an elegant manner. Elegance is a learned behavior. To refine one's conduct presupposes the development of spiritual disciplines. These practices cannot be overstated. Fruitful worship leaders practice solitude. They discover that contemplation is the only way to know God intimately. To represent Jesus to a congregation, a worship leader must be attuned to His subtle ways. The leader must sense His direction and be courageous enough to flow away from the printed agenda if necessary.

The church will be no more *adept* at honoring the Lord than the worship leader is *adroit* at waiting on the Lord, practicing solitude and meditation as well as listening for His voice, word, will, and insight.

With that said, worshipping God in spirit also refers to a spontaneous move of the Holy Spirit in a service. One of the metaphors used to image this phenomenon is a river. Entering in is a way of saying, "I'm good with what You want to teach me today, Lord Jesus. Have Your own way! You are the potter, Master. I am the clay."

As a young person doing my best to attend to the presence of the Lord, I embraced two songs that, over time, greatly affected my spiritual formation. The first song focused on the picture of a river.

There is a river that flows from deep within.

There is a fountain that frees the soul from sin.

Come to the water; there is a vast supply.

There is a river that never shall run dry.[3]

---

[3] Max and David Sapp, "There Is a River," 1969.

The river is a picture of the Lord's endless supply of grace and mercy. The river is a picture of God's Spirit, who fills us with the knowledge of His grace and mercy ushering us into His presence.

As I sang that song, I felt His presence, His power, and His love for me. He carried me through the teen years and the many transitions we all face during those tempestuous times. Although I didn't fully understand the implications of an overflowing river, singing that simple song surely filled me with peace when confused and comfort when under the stress of taking exams. I knew as I sang that He was present in my life, calming each storm I encountered, for "the Lord has His way in the whirlwind and in the storm" (Nahum 1:3). Said another way, I felt His effulgence bubbling up from deep within.

One evening during that impressionable season of my life, a talented couple who traveled in ministry came to present a concert for us. They sang a new song that has edified me from that evening until now.

Set my spirit free that I may worship Thee

Set my spirit free that I may praise Your Name.

Let all bondage go and let deliverance flow

Set my spirit free to worship Thee.[4]

At an early age, I discovered that singing drew me into His presence. And in His presence, my problems subsided. Worshipping God in spirit is a choice we all make. It allows a song to penetrate past our cognition into the deep, emotional crevices of our beings. There, in that sacred moment, God works. He performs spiritual surgery—softening our heart, healing our memories, and encouraging us amid our trials. The goal of a move of the Holy Spirit is to help us become more Christlike in attitude and decorum. When we sing, He speaks! I believe that wholeheartedly. Yet the converse is also true.

Poet Hans Christian Andersen charmingly noted, "When words fail, music starts." However, sometimes the pain of a trial is so great that we

---

[4] Charlotte Baker, "Set My Spirit Free," 1975.

simply cannot sing. But avoiding worship during a test is the wrong thing to do. As counterintuitive as that may seem, coming to church amid one's pain is precisely the right thing to do! Singing cradles a wounded traveler along the sojourn. If you just can't sing, Andersen is saying, let the music sing for you. Come and listen. Absorb. Bathe. Be submerged. Let the hot springs—so to speak—wash over your spirit with intensity. "Let the word of Christ dwell in you richly" (Colossians 3:16 NKJV).

These two songs taught me something intrinsic about singing in the spirit. God has infinite ways in which to communicate with us and help us stabilize our heartache in tough times. Sometimes while we sing, we receive an indefinable peace. Other times, we'll suddenly receive a thought never before considered. And that thought will be the key to solving a lingering problem. Still other times, we'll receive a check in our spirit not to go in one direction but in another. Direction and confirmation, peace and comfort, and the healing of memories are all matters of the heart that are relayed to our cognition while we are singing spirit songs in worship.

Real worship is that of the heart.

—Harry Ironside, revered, former pastor of Moody Church

Deep calls unto deep.

—Psalm 42:7

I would simply add one more thought. As you grow in Christ, you will find your own spirit songs to sing. The Lord will place poems, set to music, directly in your path to strengthen and uphold you just as these did for me. But until then, I encourage you to use the lyrics of my songs to serve as an altar.

Ask the Lord to refresh your spirit as you privately meditate on these poems. Ask the Lord to massage the messages of each into the very marrow of your bones. Learn their intended lessons. Gain their insightful perspective. Apply the unscripted metaphors. Rehearse their scriptural origins. Pro-activate this resource unto a deepening understanding of God's love, intentionality, and purpose for your life.

Then you will accomplish my dual objective in writing about a theology of worship. Initially I wanted to testify of how good God was—teaching me these important truths so early in life. This is how I began to learn about the ways of the Lord.

Second, I encourage you to do the same! Watch for the song that pricks your heart and gently moves you to surrender. Let songs at once encourage you and deepen your faith. This is how church musicians remain stable amid the ministry's ups and downs. This is how we mature. This is how we defeat the "wiles of the devil" (Ephesians 6:11 NKJV). Notably, as we sing and meditate on the lyrics of certain heart songs, we are emboldened to "run the race" (Hebrews 12:1; 1 Corinthians 9:24).

Worshipping God in spirit is both practical and personal. But there is more. Worshipping God in truth is a directive to know what the Bible has to say about the many features of congregational praise and worship. In the Old Testament, the Levities had specific instructions regarding the preparation and implementation of the Temple worship. While we now live under grace, it does not escape my thinking that God is nonetheless organized, thoughtful, and principled. To worship Him truthfully presupposes a commitment on our part to do "all things … decently and in order" (1 Corinthians 14:40 NKJV).

Worshipping God in truth is also a reference to worship body language, as clearly outlined in Scripture. In this instance, I believe we should study the many passages that clarify appropriate, useful body language. Body movement reinforces cognitive capacity. Noticing all the references in the Bible about using our hands, stance, and voices to honor His name is healthy and meaningful.

Joyfully being open to this process is a delightful act of obedience before the Lord (Romans 12:1–2; 2 Corinthians 10:5). For example, in the Bible, we read it is appropriate to

- lift our hands (Psalm 63:3–4);
- clap our hands (Psalm 47:1 NKJV);
- shout our praise (Psalm 22:25);
- sing spiritual songs (Colossians 3:16; Ephesians 5:19);
- kneel before the king (Philippians 2:9–10);
- bow our heads (Micah 6:6–8);

- relish a silent moment (Psalm 46:10); and
- dance for joy (Psalm 149:3).

The scriptural mandates for body language are written to aid the worshipper in attending to the presence of the Lord. Each time we move our bodies—changing a stance, lifting a hand, or altering a gesture—scientists acknowledge we reboot our brain. Our focus becomes keener, our thoughts don't waver, and endorphins burst with energy. The physicality of worship, written about so long ago, is utterly germane and reinforced by science today.

How Do We Take Corporate Worship Seriously?

At worship's core, there is enough scriptural evidence to support a congregation taking the worship presentation seriously. When it is time to sing on Sunday, we should actively enter in. And when at work or school on Monday, we should employ the full panoply of results that emanate from the rich dialogue that communing with the King—during worship—unveiled.

As we sing, you see, we become "more than conquerors!" (Romans 8:37 NKJV). We actualize the promise, "They overcame him

> *After all, what is singing if not testifying to God's goodness?*

by the blood of the Lamb and by the word [song] of their testimony" (Revelation 12:11 NKJV).

This is what makes a Christian "salt and light" (Matthew 5:13). We attend church to honor God. In the process of worship, giving God His due, we are somehow rebooted. In other words, blessing the name of the Lord results in our being refilled from what leaked out in the rough-and-tumble marketplace during the prior week. There in the daily working environment, the pushing and shoving, lying and betraying, and the every-person-for-themselves mentality are commonplace. But when we return to the sanctuary, the safest place in the universe, we are able to recuperate, forgive, retool, and "put on the whole armor of God" (Ephesians 6:11 NKJV).

More deeply, as we enter into the congregational singing, we adopt a Kingdom mind-set to respond to conflict in the opposite spirit. As we sing, we access grace.

- "Not to repay evil with evil or insult with insult. But repay evil with blessing" (1 Peter 3:9).
- "To love our enemies and pray for those who persecute us" (Matthew 5:44).
- "Not to be overcome by evil, but overcome evil with good" (Romans 12:21).

These counterintuitive responses to the so-called rat race are the direct result of being intentional about our focus in worship.

In church, we often get what we expect. If we criticize the service or the pastoral staff, we will leave with a negative attitude. The work of the Lord in us will be thwarted by our misguided attention. By the same token, if we refuse to control our minds and binge on our problems, our mind will override—or virtually ignore—what the Holy Spirit wants to do internally. Please remember that the Holy Spirit is gentle. Only when we invite His comfort, on bended knee, do we find His wisdom, His counsel, and His wonder working.

Consequently, a large discussion in much of the church world today centers around the question, "Is it enough to attend church, or do we have to pay attention when we're there?" I contend that our privilege—our highest honor on this planet—is to enter in each Sunday without hesitation, criticism, or arrogance.

C. S. Lewis famously wrote about attending a church entirely frustrated by the choice of repertoire, saying,

> When I first became a Christian ... I thought I could do it on my own, retiring to my room and reading theology. I wouldn't go to church. I disliked very much their hymns which I considered to be fifth-rate poems set to sixth-rate music. But as I went on I saw the great merit of it ... I realized that the hymns were being sung with devotion and benefit by an old saint. in elastic-side boots in the

opposite pew, and then you realize that you aren't fit to clean those boots. It gets you out of your solitary conceit.

Participative worship has the capacity to strip our pride away. This is useful. Pride, you see, leaves little space in our heart for the Lord. But when we embrace humility—singing when asked—we become agile in the spiritual realm, open to being taught about the things of God. Only then can a worship encounter illumine our path forward.

So often it seems that Christians struggle with the tongue. They readily judge others while giving themselves a break. But worship flattens the turf for all of us. To worship is to realize that no one is better than another. When we can love the unlovely, give willingly to those who are less fortunate, or surrender our pride for His peace, as C. S. Lewis described, worship becomes beautiful beyond description. It is wholesome not to say everything we think; to learn to edit our thoughts and control our tongue. This is one way to prepare for worship. Before walking onto the chancel, simply ask forgiveness for any time in which you spoke out of turn. To that end, self-control related issues are serious matters about which to pray days prior to a worship encounter. Keeping the heart soft is a matter of becoming Christlike. If we can reflect Jesus on Sunday rather than our flesh, worship becomes sweeter not to mention impactful.

I love to worship the Lord. Singing in church is, for me, a warm shower after a dusty journey. It is a moment of peace amid turbulence. There are times in which the spirit of worship attacks hell with devastation, fortifying a weary believer during a time of doubt, fear, or loneliness.

St. Paul understood this. He was shipwrecked, beaten, jailed, and treated without respect on many occasions. In the middle of his trials though, he gained insight into surviving life's horrors, its unrelenting perplexities. And he wrote that worship strengthens the soul in the "endurance of hardship" (2 Timothy 2:3 NKJV).

> *Thankfully, congregational singing, offered from a biblical perspective, offers God's hug, Jesus's smile, and the Holy Spirit's guidance.*

Clearly I have learned that authentic worship is utterly dialogical. This is a fundamental tenet of a comprehensive theology of worship. That is why I am so fervent about incorporating the scripture "forsake not the assembling of yourselves together" (Hebrews 10:25) into this chapter. We can be edified by a YouTube video or a pastor's podcast to be sure. But one cannot sit at home and possibly find the same kind of spiritual regeneration that comes to a zealous, unified singing home church or sanctuary of believers by streaming alone. There is power in public worship.

But one has to be there to gain access to its fruits. The fruit of worship begins with unity: the common understanding that when we participate, something in heaven shakes loose. Unity then is the springboard for the anointing. And the anointing breaks the bonds of deception, discouragement, and demonic oppression.

"They that wait upon the Lord shall renew their strength. They shall mount up with wings, as eagles. They shall run and not get weary; they shall walk and not faint. Teach me, Lord; teach me, Lord, to wait" (Isaiah 40:31, text to an old spiritual as well).

Waiting, like worshipping, works!

As a veteran worship leader, I have found great resonance in the writings of spiritual directors like Henri Nouwen, Thomas Merton, and Richard Rohr. These godly men have devoted their lives to contemplation and solitude. They were taken behind the veil. Hence, their writings on matters relating to church worship explode with insight, valuable commentary, and discernment.

One such insight comes from the pen of Henri Nouwen. "The purpose of spiritual reading [and singing] is not to master knowledge or information, but to let God's Spirit master us. Strange as it may sound, spiritual reading [and singing] means to let ourselves be read by God. We should read and sing with spiritual attentiveness and wonder."

Worshipping God in spirit and in truth is a holy endeavor. The understandings therein will pay dividends galore if you and I will apply the principles of this scripture to our weekly commitment to give our best to the Master. He clearly gave His best for us on the cross of Calvary.

The prominent author, James F. White, chides, "Spirit without truth is helpless, while truth without spirit is a 'theology without fire!'"

It is the pleasing of God that is at the heart of worship.

—R.C. Sproul

Seeds from the Core

1. A theology of worship is a codified statement of what God has said about our praise and worship.
2. The songs of worship should reflect the taste of all the generations in the church.
3. Singing welcomes the presence of the Lord.

Above all other traits, Kingdom people are people of worship.

—Jack W. Hayford

CHAPTER 2

AT THE CORE: PART 2

Scripture describes what worship is about. First and foremost worship was created to honor God Himself. It is the right thing for us—His subjects—to do. Somehow in western church culture we have confused what is sacred with what is trendy. The singing of the congregation is not about us—our preferences, problems, or personal needs. Certainly those matters are important to Jesus, and once His presence is established, He enters the sanctuary with abundant provision to bring healing to every area of brokenness we possess. But according to the Word, worship begins by ministering to the Lord. To that end, welcoming Him through musical praise and verbal adoration is our starting point—our plumb line. When we worship we put God, not ourselves, first. David, the Old Testament king, wrote the majority of the Psalms with that clear understanding in mind. Praise proceeds petition.

Old Testament Worship Proclamations

I have spent my life applying the worship-related truths from three additional scriptures. They come from the book of the Psalms. Each text builds on the former. And each awakened a teachable moment in my pilgrimage, after which I would never again be the same. It is my sincere hope that your walk with Jesus will include similar moments of internalizing the following.

Play Skillfully ...

One of my earliest encounters with Jesus occurred while reading Psalm 33. In that scripture, verse 3, is this command, "play skillfully" (NKJV). It is basic. It is honest. And it is unmistakably clear. For the reality of an artist's life is this: there is no substitute for technique. If Jesus died on a cross for our sin, certainly we can endure the rigor of practice in order to play skillfully for Him. Nothing is to be gained by sloppiness or digital inaccuracies.

I submitted to this discipline. I discovered that skill under the anointing brings pleasure to our Creator. It was, in effect, my sacrifice of praise. We have only this present life to make the most of our talent. We will live the years necessary to do so, either being disciplined or being lazy. The choice is ours. For me, there was no choice at all! I wanted to do my best for the Kingdom. Won't you?

One will never regret practicing an instrument rigorously. I have met lots of people who wish they had! I am reminded of the refrain from the prophet, "Choose whom you will serve. As for me and my house [church], we will serve the Lord" (Joshua 24:15).

My musical training was inextricably linked to my devotion to Jesus. And at this juncture of my life, the rigor proved not only worthwhile but the catalyst for a wonderfully exciting ride. My hope for you, dear reader, is that you will internalize the message of Psalm 33:3 as I have.

Don't bury or blur your talent. Be responsible. Number your days. Set the bar high. Excellence is not only a mind-set but a lifestyle. Work hard. Live in rarified air! Finally do your best. Our Master did His best on the cross for you and me.

Make His Praise Glorious ...

In Psalm 66:2, I found the next step in a theology of worship. Making praise glorious is to throw your being—full throttle, 100 percent—into the process. Making praise glorious is all about memorability. Any event that becomes memorable, be it a birthday party, a wedding ceremony, or a graduation celebration, requires planning, financial backing, and industry.

It takes time to do the hard work behind the scenes. It takes resources to finance equipment, repertoire, and instruments. It takes hard work to wait on God, practice, and present worship with authenticity.

Moreover, making praise glorious involves attention to detail. There is no substitute for a commitment to excellence in the work of ministry. We should strive to avoid ruts and minimalize sameness or stylistic favoritism. Instead we should embrace the singing of new songs and old songs presented in new ways. For scriptures mention the value of singing a new song dozens of times.

There is something special about newness. A new outfit, a new piece of jewelry, and a new vehicle all give a person a lift! (No pun intended!) Similarly, singing a new song gives a congregation a new vocabulary with which to offer praise.

Variety is the spice of life. Keeping our relationship with the Lord vital presupposes discovering new ways of expressing our love, gratitude, and needs. As a husband searches for new ways to communicate his love for his wife, so a worship leader should intentionally think about incorporating new songs—in new ways—to honor our Lord. Making His praise glorious, as evidenced by a celebration of Jesus in which personal devotion, creative planning, and generosity in relationships, are baked into the presentation.

I am amazed by how many memories I have in which I toiled to keep my worship leading—or my public speaking—fresh.

For me, the common thread is perhaps surprising. After finding a new song, rehearsing it with my team, folding it into a flow of other songs thematically—or—after developing a text for a devotional or a sermon, maintaining my spiritual disciplines, and finding the right story for the application phase—I would always lay my presentation down. Literally I would say, "Lord, establish the work of my hands" (Psalm 90:17).

Then when I least expected it, a brand-new procedure would suddenly breeze past my brain. Problem resolved! Or in real time during a live service, a burst of creativity would suddenly arrest my attention.

Over time I learned to go with the revelation, the Spirit-formed improvisation. As unusual as this may sound, depending on the Holy Spirit with regard to sudden revelations kept my ministry on the cutting edge.

We cannot possibly know who on any given Sunday needs comfort, direction, or healing. If the worship leader is sensitive to the voice of the Lord, a sudden impression amid the planned songs may come. In that moment of grace, I would instantly modify the plan. Maybe I would linger a bit longer on the song currently being sung. Perhaps I would add another song to the mix. Or maybe I would interrupt the flow with a word of encouragement, of exhortation. More often than not, that simple modification (instant in season) would directly minister to a wounded, discouraged, or troubled congregant as he or she would tell me after the fact.

Learning the voice of the Spirit while in public is a learned behavior. At first, one wonders if the impression is just ego. But after walking with the Lord for a season, a leader begins to recognize the voice of the Shepherd. And if the impression is of the Lord, a peace will instantly ensue as the worship leader moves into the flow of the Spirit. Trust the Shepherd's voice, for trust trumps a worship leader's fear of the unknown.

To this day, I depend upon the working of the Holy Spirit when I am in public ministry. Listening is underrated in courses on ministry methods in my view. The last-minute incursion of Spirit-led data is life-saving from a congregational perspective.

The Mountains Melt Like Wax

This descriptive promise found in Psalm 97: 5 declares a powerful truth. The pursuit of God's presence is well worth the sacrifice—the appropriate mindset to prepare our hearts before offering our opening songs of praise. When God is honored and Jesus is welcomed on the wings of a song, the Holy Spirit's ministry begins to brood. What a marvel! In that milieu, often referred to as the presence of the Lord, the needs of the people submit to the Master's tender touch. Mountains—however big—dissipate when Jesus looks our way. The key, though, is a proper understanding and subsequent discipline to carefully nurture the song of praise in the opening moments of a worship service. Scripture also declares, "In [His] Presence is fullness of joy" (Psalm 16:11). I cannot fully describe the emotion I feel as I begin a worship encounter and observe, song by song, how a congregation awakens to the entrance of the King. Moods shift. Expressions lighten. Stony hearts soften.

The composer Geron Davis aptly wrote, "In the presence of Jehovah, God Almighty, Prince of Peace, Troubles vanish. Hearts are mended, In the Presence of the King."

If you and I can understand these phenomena and stay in the groove of Holy Spirit fullness, our church will flourish no matter the politics, tumult, or economy of the country in which we live.

New Testament Worship Affirmation

My final verse of motivation with regard to leading worship is found in the New Testament. In James 4:8, we read, "Draw near to God and He will draw near to you" (NKJV).

Draw Near ...

He is the King. We are His servants. Our responsibility is to take the initiative. For worship on Sunday is all about us ministering to the Lord. Here is the secret: if we will take the first step, He'll respond with two!

Many come to church out of obligation, tradition, or peer pressure. Hence, they tend to observe rather than participate. However, the New Testament speaks about taking initiative. The worship leader's demeanor has great import in overcoming the inertia of an apathetic congregant.

As such, being skillful starts the ball rolling. Choosing to make the praise we offer truly glorious picks up the pace. Believing, contending, expecting not only add fuel to the fire but offer the green light for Him to enter and melt our problems, adding to the celebration. Our hopes are rekindled. Our fears are banished. Our dreams take on the real possibility of accomplishment. All is well when the Lord arrives on the wings of a song!

Quoting His Word under our breath, "Lord, I'm here for You. Won't You come and be blessed by our offerings of song?" opens the windows of heaven!

These scriptures informed my choices throughout the week. I thought of them as I planned, rehearsed, and presented worship. I took a step toward the Lord each time I led. My team and I made the choice in rehearsal to apply a spirit of excellence to our music and an enthusiasm to make the praise as memorable as possible on the Lord's Day.

Nonetheless, it was Jesus, Lord of the Church, who melted mountains and ministered grace to the congregation. He, in fact, "established the work of our hands" (Psalm 90:17).

Please notice the protocol of His anointing. First, we complete our due diligence. No detail is unimportant. Then we pray the prayer of faith, and afterward, He melts mountains!

Practical Applications of a Theology of Worship

I believe that worship stands in an equal proximity to the pastor's sermon and the Holy Communion in its divine ability to nurture, edify, and concretize the soul. As we sing, listen, and partake, we are made whole.

The power of three! John 15 (selected verses) summarizes some of what Jesus taught.

> I am the true vine, and My Father is the gardener. He prunes so that every branch will be even more fruitful. No branch can bear fruit by itself; it must remain in the vine. Neither can you bear fruit unless you remain in me. Apart from me you can do nothing. If you remain in me and my words remain in you, ask what you wish And it will be given you. This is to my Father's glory, that you bear much fruit, Showing yourselves to be my disciples.

Phrase	Application
I am the true vine	Authentic worship will always glorify Jesus, Lord of the Church.
No branch can bear fruit by itself	Worship cannot be observed on a computer screen at home and produce the same outcome as being present with like-minded Christ followers in the sanctuary.

Apart from me you can do nothing	In worship we are bolstered to face the trials, tests, and temptations of life victoriously. We are also replenished from the ways in which we leak the promises of Christ combating the stresses of life.
This is my Father's glory	As we enter in, we give Him the glory due His name while simultaneously receiving strength to pass the test and be a testimony to those in need around us.

At worship's core, the parable of the vine and branches makes sense.

Worship keeps us hooked in. Worship banishes the lies of the adversary. Worship reinforces our knowledge of Kingdom mentality. As we sing, we are transformed "by the renewing of our minds" (Romans 12:2).

Therefore, the worship leader must be intentional in choosing songs not only for their musical essence but for their lyrical merit. All the generations present in a church are counting on us to create musical love letters for them to read (sing) to Jesus in corporate worship. If we choose the right song for the right moment, we grow! By the same token, if we only sing the songs that a particular demographic enjoys, to the chagrin of the rest of the flock, we obtain mixed results at best. This is ineffectual.

I believe the effective worship encounter moves us from glory to glory. While singing—lost in His presence—we grow stronger like athletes working out in the gym. This strength is multifaceted.

We grow more like Him as we sing songs about Him. We discover keys to resolve problems, cope with irregular people, or manage our resources as we sing to Him. We gain insight into how to listen more attentively to His voice, thereby avoiding traps and temptations that cause us to stumble, as we commit to sing for Him.

Our faith in His ability to care for us—in every test and trial—becomes more dominant than the fear that frequently accompanies those who do enter in to worship. I always tell those in my workshops, "If you mumble on Sunday, you'll stumble on Monday!" Said another way, as I learned how to choose songs that edified, Jesus used those words to apply the Bible's many lists of character and conduct while the congregation sang.

Let me explain. The biblical lists of character and conduct are an excellent straightedge for determining the merit of a new song or hymn tune. We become what we sing. For a variety of overt and covert reasons, then the songs worship leaders choose, weeks before presentation, deeply affect the very lives of the congregation we serve.

> *As we sing, we will become self-disciplined. We will grow in Christlikeness. We will overcome!*

As a worship leader, the overt rationale for song selection is that they possess either the seeds of praise or the seeds of spiritual formation. These all-important lyrical decisions create the behavioral criteria for a fruitful Christian life. If you and I decide to make each biblical list a part of our lifestyle, reinforced through the worship song material we sing each week, we have the potential to not only achieve mastery over temptation but spiritual maturity as well.

The covert reason for examining the biblical lists for character and conduct has to do with creating a devotional curriculum, a cataclysm if you will, for worship team devotions in the rehearsal environment. Humans do not fall out of the womb knowing how to properly conduct our lives without instruction from our parents. Similarly, worship team members do not know how to conduct their ministry life without instruction from their pastor or worship leader.

Where does a worship leader find resources from which to build a year's devotions—for the rehearsal? From the biblical lists! A rehearsal is not only designed to learn repertoire for the Sunday worship encounter but to practice the very Christianity about which they sing. As the singers study the Word of God during a devotional in rehearsal, their spirits unify. In one accord, they rise to lead the congregation the following Sunday. Scripture confirms this conviction.

In John 8:31–32, we read, "If ye continue in my word, then are ye my disciples indeed; and ye shall know the truth, and the truth shall make you free" (KJV). Singing songs and hymns of lyrical depth is one of the salient ways in which a congregation embraces spiritual formation. We sing our songs. As we sing, we memorize and internalize the lyrics—full of grace and truth! Having memorized the lyrics, we then bring the tunes to work with us. We hum in the hall. We hum in the marketplace. We hum as we commute.

Then a test comes. Foremost in our thinking—just in the nick of time—we remember the godly principles of the lyrics sung in church, reinforced in our devotions, repeated during our meditations, and suddenly cause us to respond to the argument or tragedy besetting us in the opposite spirit. When an unexpected calamity strikes, the singing believer has the fortitude to respond with calm resolve. When someone despitefully uses you, the singing believer agilely adapts to praying—instant in season—for the one trying to manipulate. This is how we overcome "the way of the wound" as richly described by Richard Rohr in his landmark book, *Falling Upward.*

Congregational singing is not formatted weekly merely for tradition or liturgical purity. The congregational song is a weapon in the hand of the army of the Lord. The song is to be used both defensively and offensively. We defend the faith as we grow in spiritual formation. And we also use the song to battle the work of the adversary in an offensive posture as a need arises.

The Word says, "From the days of John the Baptist until now the Kingdom of heaven suffers violence, and the violent take it by force" (Matthew 11:12 NKJV). When the devil accuses you, sing! When he torments you, sing louder! When tragedy befalls, shout the praise!

However, if the worship leader chooses only the songs of one generation or only the pop tunes that are like cotton candy, the house has been built on sand, not on the solid rock. Dear ones, there are songs, and there are songs! Choose carefully.

> *There is a time for a violent response to chaos. Jesus Himself sweat drops of blood in prayer.*

What you sing has at once prophetic implications and applications. That is why I believe the best worship leaders may not be the trendy, most tattooed, or even those with the greatest vocal prowess. I assert that the best worship leaders are the greatest listeners! For God will always tell the "tuned in" what to sing. He did that for me on countless occasions.

The Pillars We Erect

Over the years I discovered that worship activates faith. When we sing on task, leaving our problems at the door and embracing our role as servants to our King, God Himself grows larger than our problems. Our firm acknowledgment of His ability to protect us is augmented by the unity of expression that rings in clarion fashion when the congregation sings. The effect of a congregation morphing into a choir is reminiscent of the story in 2 Chronicles 20. In this instance, a choir went before the soldiers in battle. Upon hearing the battle cry, the enemy grew in confusion and committed hari-kari. They were soundly defeated.

Worship is not only an aesthetic experience but a clarion call from singers clad in "the armor of God" marching as it were to victory. That promise is validated in the New Testament with the timeless words of St. Paul. Check out this command:

> Put on the whole armor of God, that you may be able to stand against the wiles of the devil. For we do not wrestle against flesh and blood, but against principalities, against powers, against the rulers of the darkness of this age, against spiritual hosts of wickedness in the heavenly places. (Ephesians 6:11–12 NKJV)

What are the elements of the whole armor of God?

- The Belt of Truth (v. 14)
- The Breastplate of Righteousness (v. 14b)
- Fitted feet with the readiness that comes from the gospel of peace (v. 15)
- The Shield of Faith (v. 16)
- The Helmet of Salvation (v. 17)
- The Sword of the Spirit (v. 17b)

The passage ends with two caveats: Pray [sing] in the Spirit (v. 18). Be Alert! (v. 18b).

Behind the veil of worship, a battle rages for the souls of the congregation we serve. Augustine said, "He who sings, prays twice!" The properties of a song are efficacious. As such, singing is an element of spiritual warfare.

Please follow my logic. At once, the opening praise sets the stage for the entrance of the Lord. Carefully chosen songs are poised to stimulate a release of the flow of the Spirit, minister to the felt needs of the people, bind up their wounds, clarify their purpose, edify with faith, and beat back the adversary's lying minions. "The battlefield of the mind," as Joyce Meyer notes, is at stake. And the song of the Lord cleanses the heart and gives us all a restart.

As we sing, according to Scripture, we put on the armor of God. Each congregant needs a different element dependent

Worship is potent in the Spirit realm.

on his or her unique circumstance. This is no problem for the Creator of the universe. Some need peace. Others need a promise. Still more need protection. All these situations are addressed as we sing.

Still, more are experiencing a crisis of faith and need to reaffirm the truth of the gospel. And then there are those among us who haven't made a commitment of faith. Perhaps the perfect time for an altar call is right in the middle of a worship encounter.

What I love about the Bible is how balanced its truth is—Old and New Testaments. Stories in the Old Testament have references to passages in the New Testament. The Bible is perfectly symmetrical.

To conclude this chapter, I would like to draw two conclusions. If a worship leader will absorb the symmetrical beauty of the biblical lists for character and conduct as noted below, both for lyrical song search and worship team devotional material, the worship of the church will blossom. Please review these lists.

- **The Old Testament:** Ten Commandments, Seven Deadly Sins, and Three Things God Requires
- **The New Testament:** Beatitudes, Fruit of the Spirit, and Think on These Things

Second, I complete my remarks with the inclusion of two insightful quotations assuring my plumb line is straight. These statements are power-packed with truth, vision, and high purpose. My life as a worship leader has been enhanced not only by keeping the biblical lists for character and conduct fresh in my mind but by meditating on the scholarship of godly men and women who went before me.

These remarks call me to a circumspect goal of taking the work of the ministry seriously. Planning and facilitating worship is, after all, not about my aesthetics or my talents. This sacred office of leading worship is about caring for the flock by choosing songs that will nurture their growth and development, not merely entertain their preferences.

Let us all rise to accept our calling and thereby dismiss the distractions that clang so loudly in these contemporary times of social media influence.

Worship is:

- *To quicken the conscience by the holiness of God*
- *To feed the mind with the truth of God*
- *To purge the imagination by the beauty of God*
- *To open the heart to the love of God*
- *To devote the will to the purpose of God.*

—William Temple

A worship service, ideally speaking, is designed to invoke:

- *A recognition of majesty*
- *A sudden, rather blunt awareness of one's own unworthiness*
- *A declaration of deep repentance*
- *A transaction of forgiveness and absolution*
- *A hearing of God's voice as one's life is freshened and redirected.*

—Gordon MacDonald

These are the constructs that frame this workable theology of worship.

I freely give them to you for I believe, "A candle that lights another loses nothing!"[5]

Seeds from the Core

1. Worship is primarily about giving God the worth He truly deserves.
2. Worship is a participative exercise, not a concert we dutifully observe.
3. Worship hears God afresh.

---

[5] This statement was written by Father Frank Keller

It's not the state of the art, but the state of the heart that matters most to God.

—Tom Brooks

CHAPTER 3

TWO OR THREE

His name was Max. He was a marine who fought in Vietnam. We could not have been more opposite. I am a right-brained musician; he's a left-brained financier. After the war, he became a successful banker. When we met, he was the CFO of our church in Los Angeles, The Church On The Way. Somehow in spite of polar opposite career paths, we became fast friends. Max had a quaint Southern charm, prized sports of all kinds, and for some inexplicable reason cared for me as well. Opposites attract, they say.

One Sunday after a service, he spontaneously offered one of the most treasured observations of my pastoral career. Max said, "Tom, I love when you lead worship because God speaks to me when you do. He talks to me about my kids, my finances, and the burdens of my day. I can actually hear His voice while you sing!"

Max, in his unassuming way, unveiled one of the great mysteries of Christian worship. And it is this: Jesus loves to hear us sing! When we sing, He is actually moved with delight. To that end, if the singing is from the heart—evidenced by a congregation's full-throttled engagement, unabashed—He will speak to us as we sing. In that anointed moment, He forgives, restores, and refreshes. What's more, He banishes fear, obliterates mental anguish, and reinstates grace.

> *Jesus is active when the congregation—of any size—participates.*

The unity that emerges

amid vibrant congregational singing is palpable. As a musician, I clearly understand the promise inherent in the scripture, "Forsaking not the assembling of ourselves together" (Hebrews 10:25 KJV).

Why? Because there is something irreplaceable about live singing in the sanctuary. Honestly, if you are absent, you'll not experience its requisite joy in the same way. Singing with enthusiasm in church is tantamount, I believe, to the effect of the angel choir who sang boldly on the night in which Jesus was born. Of course, that was a landmark musical offering! The angelic singing that night punctuated the line between BC and AD and was immortalized in scripture. Even so, I believe when congregations sing today as one, things change dramatically in and around us.

My wife and I live close to the Pacific Ocean. In June each year, we experience thick morning cloud cover that usually burns off by lunchtime. The sun accomplishes this feat. In the same way, when you and I attend church, amid cloudy personal circumstances, and make the choice to participate regardless, the Son burns our gloom away too! This is the great potential of a congregational song. A song is at once redemptive, dialogical, and hope-filled.

Still, I know what you must be thinking. "Tom, you may quip, 'Really!' You were the worship leader at one of the most significant American Charismatic churches of the twentieth century. Your church was close to Hollywood. There were thousands of congregants there. Your band featured prominent studio musicians! Of course the congregation sang enthusiastically. How could they not have? You just don't know my situation, Tom. There aren't enough in our fellowship to even realize four-part harmony. How is it that Jesus would even think twice about us?"

Enter the second mystery of Christian worship. Musical excellence is wonderful. But the Lord is no respecter of persons. His grace is not limited to certain lofty locations known around the world. And more importantly, the Bible says, "Do not despise the day of a small beginnings" (Zechariah 4:10).

There are great promises of scripture throughout the Word of God to concretize what I am suggesting. Follow the supportive biblical narrative, "Where two or three are gathered together in My name, I am there in the midst of them" (Matthew 18:20 NKJV).

These words of Jesus are an assurance for all church pastors to claim.

They signify His heart for the gathering of believers worldwide. I want to be clear. Jesus is not moved by glitz and glamour in worship encounters as He is moved by integrity of heart. His heart melts for those who, under difficult circumstances, courageously offer the sacrifice of praise. Simplicity with purity delights the Master. Jesus looks to the heart; mankind looks to the art. This was observed throughout His earthly ministry. The outcast, the disenfranchised, those in need, and those for whom the Pharisees disregarded always captured the attention of Jesus.

Be encouraged, my dear colleague. He promises never to leave us. He looks on us with compassion. The feelings of our infirmity move Him. His ways are a marvel. He is with you no matter your church's accouterments.

Moses' life and ministry are a prime example of what I am describing. God said, "Take your shoes off your feet. For the place where you are standing is holy ground" (Exodus 3:5). Moses was asked to take off his shoes in the presence of the burning bush. Moses was in an arid, sandy desert at the time. There were no marble floors or gentle air-conditioning. What mattered was God's love for the future leader.

If you find yourself in a remote locale without the amenities of the twenty-first century but with a heart for God, be assured on the basis of scripture that your heart cry is being heard. Then God said, "Build altars in the places I tell you, and I will come and bless you there" (Exodus 20:24).

This affirmation of this divine call to duty, replete with the promise of God to bless us there, is momentous. Once again, the locale for building altars in Moses' era was outdoors. The structures were unpolished. God was literally blessing His people amid piles of rocks. Wherever He calls you and me becomes holy ground simply because of His Word—not because of the location's notoriety or comfort. The blessings found in the church where you serve, dear leader, are generated because of His favor with respect to your obedience. If you are authentic there, He will come!

In the New Testament, Paul and Silas also found themselves in a strange place for a visitation from the Lord. About midnight, Paul and Silas were in prison singing. Suddenly an angel appeared. The gates flew open, and everybody's chains fell loose (Acts 16:25–26). How extraordinary! Can you see it?

About midnight, these two godly men in their sixties began to sing. I would have been sound asleep by then! But the love of the Lord was pulsating in their veins, and they had no choice but to sing! What is so awe-inspiring is that their song invoked the miracle-working power of the Lord. Suddenly in that dark, dank prison cell, the Holy Spirit amplified their voices until physical matter—walls, doors, and chains—could not withstand the sheer velocity of God's pleasure.

The locked prison doors flew open! The prisoner's chains lost their brassy grip. The loud clanging was eerily jarring. Horrified, the prison guard rose in fear. He panicked, picking up his sword to commit suicide. But Paul, instant in season, led the guard to faith in Christ. Selah!

Today in my worship seminars, I will frequently remind pastoral musicians about the great possibilities inherent in leading congregations in the songs of worship, as Paul and Silas practiced, until the prison doors of addiction and forgiveness swing wide open. The chains of bitterness and temptation dramatically fall to the ground! The same power in the songs of Paul and Silas reside in the church today. If only we believed. If only we contended as they.

Pastor, the prison cell of old contained only two! If one can put a thousand to flight and two can put ten thousand, how many can your home church expel in the spirit realm? "'For [it is] not by strength nor by power, but by My Spirit,' says the Lord of All" (Zechariah 4:6).

Thinking about God blessing small groups of people in lesser than ideal places made me reflect further about biblical precedence.

- God met Shadrach, Meshach, and Abednego in the fiery furnace.
- God blessed Daniel in the Lion's Den.
- God ministered grace to Elijah after his brutal encounter with Jezebel.
- God empowered the widow's mite in a small apartment.
- Jesus touched Lazarus, dead at the time, in a home environment.
- Jesus attended to Mary and Martha in their home.
- Jesus convened the twelve for the Last Supper around a dining room table.
- Jesus was seen after His resurrection talking with two on the dusty Emmaus road.

I am reminded of the gospel refrain, "It matters to Him about you."[6] It's never about what you wear, where you live, or even about the relative notoriety your home church may enjoy. The Bible is chock full of poor widows who impressed prophets and weary persons who found healing by "troubled water." What is more, who could forget the woman who touched the hem of His garment amid the hectic crowd? It's about a sincere heart cry that says, "I need You, Lord."

For a number of years after my first tenure in Los Angeles, I was invited to serve as national director of music for a Midwestern-based denomination. My portfolio was to develop teaching materials and offer pastoral care for the worship leaders of that international church. I traveled constantly. Since the headquarters of that fellowship was located in a small town in the center of the United States, I took a commuter flight early each Friday morning to either Chicago or Dallas. There I would take a much larger jet to my destination for weekend ministry.

Before dawn, I would often arrive at the small regional airport to check in. I would walk down a brick-walled hallway toward the gate area. On the wall was a map of the world, which was backlit. The light behind the map mechanically followed the pathway of the sun from east to west. Most mornings, the United States of America was still dark while Europe, the Middle East, and Asia were glowing. I would always pause in wonder.

Quietly I would inquire of the Lord, "Dear Jesus, where around the world will You be welcomed by praise on Sunday?" I remember the dual sense of ache and awe. Some churches get it. Others just do not. "In New Deli, for example, which church will invite Your Presence through their heartfelt song? In Cairo or Paris, Berlin or London, Lord, who understands the value of a song's potential to entreat Your presence?"

I came to imagine that as the sun illumined the pathway for the Son I felt so badly for the churches stuck in traditions or liturgies that missed the mark. That revelation captured my thinking as I traveled. Today, all these years later, wherever I am invited to lead worship or speak, I am reminded of the path of the sun—as pictured by that backlit map in the simply appointed, red-bricked airport hallway.

Put simply, Jesus loves all of humanity. There is great hope for your church, your small setting, which, by virtue of protection, you have to

---

[6] Audrey Mieir, "It Matters to Him," 1959.

keep confidential or your recent appointment to a cathedral in a world-class venue. If the congregation you serve can grasp their significance and choose to enter in each time they gather and sing, Jesus will appear with "healing in His wings" (Malachi 4:2).

The mystery of worship has little to do with locale, but everything to do with one's avid participation. Victory comes as we sing loudly,

The songs of the redeemed

The songs of each generation

The songs of all nations

In every idiom, in every tempo

In every language, or in the Spirit

With instruments, or beautifully acapella

On our knees, or standing boldly before the Throne

A la Psalm 150, "Let everything that has breath praise the Lord,

Praise Ye The Lord!"

As we sing, let all expect the unexpected! Let everybody hear the clarion call—with attention to detail—and fulfill the promise of congregational attendance. If we will sing, He will appear!

From the rising of the sun in the east to its setting in the west, let the name of the Lord be praised. Sing! Sing to the Lord.

Where two or three are gathered …

In the place where I tell you …

Taking off your shoes …

At midnight …

In Christian literature, there is no place in which the concept of vibrant congregational singing is more clearly demonstrated than in the venerable treatise by C. S. Lewis, *The Screwtape Letters*. My family and I saw a play based on that book several years ago in New York City. The theatre itself was small, but the impact on us was huge.

In the second act, the colonel in hell's army warned his minions to distract the young new believer, Christian, from attending a church service. What happened next is among the most important revelations about worship's importance I have ever encountered.

Christian, the protagonist, is observed going to church. Try as he might, the demon neophyte couldn't discourage him along the journey. Suddenly the congregation began to sing "the song of the redeemed." Christian joins in. The subsequent scene staged in the office of the demon colonel was unforgettable.

With the singing of the congregation in the background, hell suddenly erupted in sheer chaos. The colonel's office began to shake as if a volcano were spewing hot lava. The minions shrieked. The chairs danced. The lights flickered. The colonel screamed in anger but to no avail. For the song in the church, sanctuary beat back the adversary's attempts to discourage. At the end of the day, there was nothing hell could do to stop the advance of the believer's unified faith. Clearly a singing sanctuary is the safest place in all the world to be!

Exiting the off-Broadway theater, we were all mesmerized, awe-inspired, and simply captivated by the play's unforgettable revelation. The depiction of C. S. Lewis' portrayal of the visceral power of a gospel song on the adversary was forever imprinted on my brain. My worldview solidified. Hope rose. Inspired songs just change everything! The sanctuary is an important place for believers to do business in the spirit realm. Songs matter.

> *It's not the state of the art, but the state of the heart that matters most to God.*

So do you, my dear reader. No matter where you are, Jesus is interested in you as a catalyst for worship. Every home church is valuable from heaven's point of view. No beginning is too small; no fresh start is too simple. Don't give up! Don't lose heart! Put simply, draw near to God, and He will draw near to you (James 4:8). In all earnest, I implore you to read on. Investigate what I am proposing.

Seeds at the Core

1. Our heavenly Father loves it when we sing. A song is at once an invitation, a dialogue, and a source of comfort and hope.
2. Our Lord Jesus is no respecter of persons. He attends to the needs of all who call on His name, in small settings or large.
3. The avid participation of a congregation—entering in—summons the presence of the King!
4. It's not the state of the art, but the state of the heart that matters most to God.

If we don't have a hidden life in God, our public life for God cannot bear fruit.

—Henri Nouwen

CHAPTER 4

MY JOURNEY

The proficiencies of a worship leader are emblematic of a three-sided stool. Imagine the first leg representing matters of musical mastery. Another signifies the many political considerations involved in serving a pastor, colleagues, volunteers, and church family. Getting along with people is essential in the work of ministry. That leaves a third leg to symbolize the elements of spiritual formation. Each leg matters. Notably, the stool will fall if one leg is weak, somehow shorter than the others, or comes unglued by heavy pressure placed on the stool. To serve the needs of the owner, the stool must balance on all three legs. Creating a fine stool takes time.

My development as a pastoral musician took place over many years. Initially there was a musical process. Second, I was fortunate enough to serve with a pastor who, in those formidable years, cared enough to disciple a young staff. His name was Earl Baldwin. Concurrently I began a lifelong pursuit to read, developed an ear for the Holy Spirit, and made profound mistakes. Not only was my pastor considerate, the congregation was patient. Third, there came a time where growth occurred through the process of networking with like-minded men and women from churches around the country. Finally I was invited to join the pastoral team of The Church On The Way. It was there that I met Jack Hayford, the megachurch vanguard. His touch upon my ministry was catalytic.

From this brief introduction, it is my hope that you will extrapolate a principle of Kingdom life: Where God calls, He provides. He is an able guide. He is "a friend who stays closer than a brother" (Proverbs 18:24). When we lack wisdom, He supplies. When betrayed by a friend, He comforts. I can boldly attest, having completed forty years of pastoral ministry, He was there all the time! He will be there for you as well. Here are excerpts of my experience studying the art of leading worship.

Three in a Row

While an undergraduate in Baltimore, I won a summer fellowship to teach at-risk high school students at a music camp on campus. While commuting to the university one muggy summer morning, I remember hearing a radio announcer broadcast a change in programming. "From today on," he said, "never less than three in a row! There will be fewer commercials, less interruptions, and more of the kind of music you love, right here, on our station."

The campaign spread like wildfire! The new marketing idea became enormously popular. How much more enjoyable it was to hear a song end and another begin without ridiculous commentary or multiple commercials.

Over that summer, I felt the Lord impressing me to introduce something similar in church. After the morning hymn, I began to add two or three worship songs of similar style to the congregation without talking in between. The flow of songs became more and more comfortable. Soon the congregation was entering in more robustly. I discovered that my silence in between songs enhanced the congregation's intimacy with the Lord. In church, silence is golden.

Sometime later, a congregant gave me a periodical in which there was a quotation by Soren Kierkegaard.

The Kierkegaard Quotation

The Danish philosopher wrote, "Too often we see the ministers and musicians as the performers and the congregation as the audience. Rather, we should see God as the audience, the congregation as the performers and the ministers and musicians as prompters assisting the congregation in doing their part."

God as the audience? The congregation as the performers? The ministers and musicians as prompters?

After a lot of soul-searching, I began to understand more acutely the cluster of challenges in leading authentic worship. For example,

I became sensitive to disappear so Jesus could appear. The chancel is not a stage. My presentation did not require "blue suede shoes." I also found ways to stop showing off so He could show up! Large, unexpected modulations or placing the key center of a ballad in the tenor range was not appropriate here. Keeping modulations simple and keys in the range of the congregation were more important than trying to impress the congregation. Minimalizing extraneous comments helped to improve their level of participation. We were making progress!

I chose to strengthen my quiet time to listen more intently in private so I could function with greater agility in public. I discovered that my private walk informed my public ministry. One growing edge in the process of leading worship, for those who are inexperienced, is found in comingling the need to listen before planning, rehearse before presenting, yield to the Holy Spirit while presenting, and read the move of the Spirit more precisely.

I always had a plan, a sequence of songs, but I grew to sing through the song sequence gingerly. For example, there were moments when the congregation needed to linger, to repeat a lyric more often than I had rehearsed. God was working. His interaction with the hurting and oppressed was taking a little longer than usual. There were other times when my last prepared song somehow wasn't enough. The mood of the room turned celebratory, and the congregation needed to pop for joy! So we'd spontaneously add a "sugar stick" as the proverbial roof came off the hinges.

There is an element of improvisation that is critical for worship leaders to accommodate as they move in the Spirit. Worship, when leader and congregant are in one accord, is one of the most gratifying experiences in life. Just as it takes a lifetime to master jazz, so too, leading worship effectively requires weekly devotion, a careful sensitivity with the selection of repertoire, and an instant-in-season mentality during the actual encounter.

Over the years of my early ministry, I became sensitive to God's voice in my morning quiet time before ever putting pencil to paper. All these years later, regardless of the size of the venue for which I've been invited to lead, I still bow my knee and inquire of the Lord before planning.

My Prayer

"Lord, what can I sing just for You? What do the people need from Your hand, Lord?"

If we bless the Lord in the opening segment of worship, giving Him the honor due His name, those moments enthusiastically sung by a unified congregation invite His presence. Following the robust singing, it would be appropriate to offer an invocation, a greeting and the articulation of an important event or announcement. Then, of course, a succinct transition would cue the congregation of worship's second phase—the songs of intimacy, felt need and adoration. These tender moments are designed to bind up the wounds of the brokenhearted, mend the war-torn memories of the victimized, forgive the sins of the repentant and impart wisdom to the ones making landmark decisions in the days ahead. If the myriad of details behind the scenes are carefully and prayerfully managed, this time is golden for the people of God. Amid the songs of the second phase of worship, the Holy Spirit moves, the Lord Jesus heals and transformations bloom like a well-watered garden. You see, our Lord is ever mindful. His hand is not weak. His wisdom is spot-on. He is moved with compassion when we honor His name prior to asking for His help or healing touch. Oh, to choose the right songs in order to effectively plug into Almighty God's plan for the congregation's restoration each week.

As a young worship leader, I was eager to master the techniques from my reading. I carefully hunted for new songs. I guided my singers and instrumentalists to present the songs of praise and worship with aplomb. We were diligent to guard our hearts and to treat a rehearsal with the same respect as a service. I observed from my pastor how to present a devotional, how to seek the anointing, maintain unity, cast vision, and uphold a shepherd's touch with regard to discipline.

Worship for Special Occasions

I also grew to understand how valuable worship became in gatherings of the church other than just for Sunday services. Examples of other events for which worship was effective include corporate gatherings for holidays, nights of healing, and prior to business meetings and rehearsals because singing to the Lord helped members transition from a day's work to the mission of the meeting. I also came to understand that personal devotions are aided by the addition of "a song, hymn, or spiritual song" (Ephesians 5:19).

What's more, holiday services for Christmas or Easter could, for example, become more festive by incorporating a soloist, dance, drama, or poem. This programmatic addition always engages a congregation's appreciation of the special holiday offered just prior to the sermon.

Keeping worship times fresh not only augments the senses but engages the mind to take note of God's goodness. Just as we enjoy new cuisine or

> *At worship's core, people value variety.*

trendy fashion, so too the scriptures teach us to "Sing a new song" (Psalm 96:1). New songs increase the church's worship vocabulary. New songs keep the congregation engaged. New songs provide teaching moments to reinforce the core values and biblical principles of worship.

As a congregation develops trust in the worship leader's authenticity, things begin to happen. I discerned the value of teaching the congregation about a worship core value when the presence of the Lord manifested in signs and wonders. You see, praise invokes His presence, but lingering in worship compels His power. A pastoral remark, in the immediacy of the moment, helps a congregation to develop an understanding of a God moment.

Our forefathers developed a useful metaphor to help describe the phenomena known as a God moment. They spoke of an imaginary window in the sanctuary's roof. These fathers and mothers of faith would carefully plan the liturgy yet always leave room for God to move at His discretion. Often amid the songs of worship, the imaginary window would open, and God would invade the church with "healing in His wings" (Malachi 4:2).

In a moment like that, my Baltimore pastor might have called for body ministry, the act of praying for the sick with the laying on of hands in a spontaneous moment of grace. In my Los Angeles experience, the pastor might have given an altar call or administered the Holy Communion. There is nothing quite as intimate as moving from adoration into Holy Communion while all are sensing His holy presence. God moments nurture congregational expectancy.

We all appreciate the kind of congregational response that emanates from wondering, "What will the Lord do next?" Expectancy in the worship encounter leads to fervency. Fervency leads to momentum, and momentum leads to growth. Being sensitive to the imaginary window makes all the difference.

Two Revelations While on the Road

During my years of denominational travel, I learned two important lessons about what it feels like to participate in worship from a congregant's perspective. For twenty-five years at that point, I led worship almost every weekend, rarely sitting in the congregation. Now I was in a different role, mentoring my colleagues. The world is a different place observing worship as opposed to leading worship.

A Timely Melody

The first revelation had to do with songwriting technique. Many worship leaders compose songs for their churches. Over time, I found myself becoming critical of songs offered to a congregation that were compositionally underdeveloped. Ironically, as I was determining a new song's merit, I found myself distracted. The effect of essentially becoming a Monday morning quarterback during church worship was minimal at first. Then I began to sense a callus forming in my heart. Soon thereafter, I perceived a slight annoyance when a worship leader would say, "I've written a song to commemorate Dr. McDonald's time with us this weekend. Would you sing it with me?"

Finally my devolution-into-frustration came to a head one Sunday while visiting a small church in New England. I drove into the town during the fall when the leaves on the trees were turning from green to shades of crimson, yellow, and a vibrant orange. The landscape was gorgeous. There was even a chill in the morning air that day. What a quintessential moment!

The service took place in an old stone chapel in the center of the town square. The building must have been 150 years old. The floors creaked. The pews were uncomfortable, and the gorgeous pipe organ needed to be serviced. Nonetheless, I fell in love. As I walked into the nave, I noticed that the sunshine was gently peeking through the stained-glass windows, creating a faint rainbowlike glow in the sanctuary. The church looked so pristine, like a scene from an old movie. I was just delighted. And then it happened.

The service began with the singing of the theme song from Whoopi Goldberg's comedy, *Sister Act*. I couldn't believe it! The worship leader had actually rewritten the lyrics and added distracting choreography. It was quite unbecoming. I would find out later their interpretation took weeks to prepare and it was designed especially for my visit!

A cognitive dissonance began to brew in my head. On the one hand, the congregation seemed overjoyed. From their perspective, their beloved worship leader had just conducted Handel's *Hallelujah Chorus*. They were so proud. Yet on the other hand, I was dismayed. Driving away after lunch with the pastor, I had an epiphany, an impression from the Lord. I felt the Lord say, "Tom, what happened in church this morning brought me delight."

I mused. The Lord was taking me deeper into an understanding of my role as national director of music. I was not there as a judge or critic. I was there as a representative of the Lord to encourage, enrich, and embolden. From heaven's vantage point, the hard work expended by the worship team hit the mark! Whenever God's children try, heaven rejoices. In Kingdom parlance, "the simple things often confound the wise" (1 Corinthians 1:27).

Remarkably, "God's ways are higher than ours" (Isaiah 55:9). Jesus looks at the heart, the motive. Unlike young fathers who, upon seeing the artwork of their preschool child and respond graciously, my evaluation of the song's relative merit completely missed the bull's-eye. It was limited in scope. The genre was simply not one I would ever choose as a call to worship.

Nonetheless, before the Lord that afternoon I repented. What is more, I decided from that day on I would remain neutral. Instead of rating a song based on my cultural references or musical preferences, I would embrace anything honestly offered to the Lord with open hands.

Moreover, I began to lecture my flock about this encounter with the Lord, saying, "It's not the style of song, but the attitude of heart that peeks heaven's attention while we sing!"

As soon as I stopped criticizing the worship and entered in without musical bias, I became enriched by what I observed across the country. Worship became precious again. I was free to commune with Jesus, ask forgiveness, sense His grace, and leave refreshed for the week ahead. My heart softened. My joy rekindled. The "still, small voice" grew more distinct. My sense of wonder, of childlike innocence in the majesty of the worship, had returned! More importantly, in a spirit of humility, I could use my story to encourage the volunteers of a local worship team to continue on their own path to creativity in the work of the ministry.

The lessons of this story are important. From that situation, I learned not to judge the worship. For if I do, I lose the opportunity to dialogue with Jesus, to sit at His feet. Evaluation comes later. In the moment when the presence of the Lord is evident, surf the wave! I also gained sensitivity to the value of letting another generation lead. Worship is as diverse as there are people on the planet. We do not necessarily have to please Tom each week.

Truthfully, some people lose out with the Lord, grow angry, and leave a church because of style-related issues. Disenfranchised, they no longer feel a part of the community because their preferences are being ignored. They resent those who incited their loss. In the spirit realm, they have unfortunately taken a third-party offense. Ironically, hell also plays a part in this onset of discouragement.

Dear reader, please make the necessary accommodations here. This dilemma is a two-sided coin. There is a worship leader responsibility and a congregational mandate. If you lead worship in a multigenerational, multicultural setting, accept the sacred responsibility to minister to all in your congregation. Keep your pulse on the style continuum. I urge you to be purposeful in your decision-making and fold in traditional hymns with the panoply of new songs so all are comforted, encouraged, and enriched in the presence of the Lord.

If you are a congregant, stay flexible. Attitude is manageable. Don't waste a worship encounter by fuming over the style or performance practice of the worship leader. For "the devil is a roaring lion seeking whom he may devour" (1 Peter 5:8). Don't fall *prey* in the place where you *pray*!

A Tender Lyric

The second revelation I experienced during my tenure as a denominational leader was equally significant. On most trips, I would speak on Friday night, lead a workshop on Saturday, and preach on Sunday morning. I chose not to lead worship each week during those years for two reasons. One reason was for vocal health. The other reason was to ensure an objective evaluation. By not leading the worship myself, I could more easily focus on my passion to help worship leaders excel.

As time passed, I became increasingly sensitive to the flow of songs as I sat by the pastor on the front row. This became a growing edge for me. In my own performance practice, my primary concern was to create musical continuity. I was interested in a smooth, seamless transition song by song. As long as the lyrics were reasonably similar, I was content. However, as a congregant, my view about lyrics shifted. I observed how lyrics either created a love letter to the Lord like fine poetry or somehow broke down into a random series of disjointed phrases. This stop-and-start process seemed to stunt intimacy. Soon I found myself either frustrated by the lack of a lyrical flow or entranced by the ability of a worship leader to gently move a congregation from outer to inner court. I made mental notes. I would never be the same again.

So in my second tenure at The Church On The Way, I not only invested prep time in choosing songs that flowed well musically, I became intentional with regard to lyrical flow as well. I regularly read the lyrics of the medley aloud beforehand so the effect on the congregation would be poetic, not disjointed.

These two experiences while traveling changed my ministry. Not only would I recommend their adaption in your professional development,

> *My big takeaway: Lyrics matter when you are a congregant!*

more saliently, I would encourage you to think about the way in which the Lord helps leaders. He uses circumstances and revelations —suddenlies, if you will—to help us mature.

This is nothing new. God used circumstances throughout the biblical narrative to guide a prophet, a king, or apostle. There was a burning bush, a floating ax head, and even a talking donkey! I am amazed by how miraculous God cares for each of us. So much so that He often goes beyond the natural, using supernatural means to answer our questions, to clarify our path.

I will forever be grateful for what I learned one fall morning in a beautifully appointed stone chapel in New England and on the front row of so many other churches across the United States.

A Collection of Definitions

Even today, I continue my quest to more deeply consecrate myself to the art of leading worship. I once read, "You can't be an interesting singer if you are not an interesting person."[7] The key to being an interesting worship leader is to become a voracious reader. That is how a pastoral musician stays on the cutting edge.

Peruse knowledge wherever possible. Study books on music theory and composition. Process biographies of great Christian leaders. Find examples of new songs online. Follow great preaching. Investigate leading church web pages. Network with other worship leaders. Maintain a curiosity about human nature, godliness, and communication theory.

Then learn to transfer that knowledge from other professions into ours. For example, what makes an individual a great salesman has bearing on how to recruit new members to your worship team or choir. Studying the rehearsal techniques of master conductors will aid the way in which we conduct a rehearsal or teach a new song to a church. This book is designed to help you comprehend the metaphor of a three-legged stool. Triangulating mastery, prowess, and formation ideas empower a worship leader to thrive.

My avocational interest in collecting definitions from scholars and poets provides insight into the myriad aspects of leading worship. I have enclosed three of my favorites for your reflection and meditation. Please take some time to discern their connotations. Each is purposeful. Each is timely. Each, dear reader, is prophetic.

Is there a space in our lives where the Spirit of God has a chance to speak or act or show up? Being contemplative ... is learning to listen in the spaces of quiet we leave for God.

—Henri Nouwen

A worship service is designed to fulfill two objectives: To serve God with our praises and to serve the congregation with His sufficiency.

—Jack Hayford

---

[7] Leland Sateren, *A Choirmaster's Miscellany* (Augsburg Press, 1978).

Many a congregation when it assembles in church must look to the angels like a muddy shore at low tide; littered with every kind of rubbish and odds-n-ends. And then the tide of worship comes in and it's all gone:

> *... The dead sea urchin and jellyfish*

> *... The paper and empty cans*

> *... The nameless bits of rubbish.*

So we are released from a narrow, selfish outlook on the universe by a common act of worship.

—Evelyn Underhill

These lessons and study habits elongated my ministry. They kept me relevant. Apply them. They'll do the same for you.

Seeds at the Core

1. The Kierkegaard model rocked my world. It changed my focus from being the focus to being a prompter of the congregation's presentation for "the audience of one."
2. My prayer before planning worship has two parts. They are important to internalize.
3. The two revelations from my years of travel involved a congregational perspective on the worship encounter. Recall my two observations.
4. If we don't have a hidden life in God, our public life for God cannot bear fruit.

POSTSCRIPT

For your meditation, please pause before reading further to let the words of the The Kierkegaard Model, once again, reverberate in your spirit.

Too often we see the ministers and musicians as the performers and the congregation as the audience. Rather, we should see God as the audience, the congregation as the performers and the ministers and musicians as prompters assisting the congregation in doing their part.

— Soren Kiekegaard

Hallowed worship stimulates, Hollow worship simulates.

—Leonard Sweet

CHAPTER 5

NEXT STEPS

Leading worship is a tricky enterprise. The presentation of songs in a service represents something of a high-wire act. There are many divergent issues to balance. At worship's core, there are points of tension to resolve and aspects of trust to build. These matters necessitate honesty, transparency, and active listening skills.

Tension comes from the facts that the senior pastor is the worship leader, the audience is not the congregation, musical skills are not as important as listening skills, worship, although sung, is not a concert, and "God commits to character not talent" (Edwin Cole).

Trust issues emanate from pastors and worship leaders not spending enough time with each other; disagreements or hurts that are left unattended; conflicts about control, micromanagement, and submission; Satan's ploys to divide the staff through subterfuge or jealousy, and the misuse of discipline when the worship leader fails or the duplicity is observed in the pastor's life.

I wish I could have read a book like this as I started to lead worship so long ago. Instead the process of my seasoning in ministry was a journey of trial and error. Yet at just the right moment Jesus always intervened. He rescued me from harmful mistakes and the escalation of misunderstandings. He taught me to listen to the "still, small voice." He softened my heart so I could forgive, move forward, and be kind toward those who were other than me.

Following are administrative concepts, interpersonal cautions, and pertinent guides to better understand the ways of the Lord. The manner with which pastors and worship leaders respond to this call-to-duty is critical to the enhancement of congregational freedom in worship, to which we all aspire.

Issues of Tension

Let's begins with potential points of tension that need to be carefully resolved.

The Senior Pastor Is the Worship Leader

I believe that God moves in a home church primarily through the appointed head. The pastor is designated to set the spiritual tone for the church. What is more, he or she is the point person for all aspects of mission and theology, pastoral care and vision casting, marketing, and service planning. The pastor's prerogative also includes the length of worship encounters and the processing of the flow of the gifts of the Holy Spirit. There are many administrative choices available to the pastor with which to manage staff members, including the worship leader.

That being said, I do not affirm a leader's choice to micromanage. This unfortunate leadership distinctive breeds contempt and conflict. Rather I assert a team approach to staff development, based on New Testament prerequisites for church interaction. In a spirit of mutual submission, new ideas should be shared freely without rebuke or retort. There should be a commitment to care about each generation's musical preferences. The team approach fosters loyalty and longevity.

The worship leader is accountable to apprise the pastor of the ongoing assignment of the music ministry. This appraisal is wide-ranging but should feature the mutual assessment of core values, personnel challenges, budgetary needs, and future projects desired. The choice of specific song selection should also be a part of an ongoing dialogue in which both leaders contribute in a spirit of transparency. As a veteran church musician, I have lived by one guiding light throughout my ministry: never surprise the pastor! Fellow worship leaders, I appeal to you to embrace these boundaries:

- Do not embarrass your leader with changes in liturgy that you have not apprised him or her about beforehand.

- Do not assume his or her taste for something novel or experimental in a worship service or other any kind of public church event without dialogue, contextualization, and a chance for the leader to ask questions first. Always talk through your vision in specificity and be open to change and/or modification.
- Do not violate his or her trust and paint walls, move chairs, or suddenly place the guitarist in the center of the worship space and expect your leader will be comfortable worshipping that weekend in a "theater-in-the-round."

If the worship leader is softhearted and the pastor is benevolent—grace-filled in manner and disposition—

Open communication signals respect.

musicians will be liberated to be creative. These collegial traits are the essential building blocks of honor and loyalty, love, and respect. Love wins.

The Audience Is Not the Congregation

This statement seems like a riddle, but I assure you it is not. Worship is presented to minister to the Lord. Recall the very opening of the Lord's Prayer, "Hallowed be Thy Name!" If we properly honor the Lord, which is our highest call, the Lord will take note. I never tire of singing praise for all the Lord has done, is doing, and will do in the future. Beyond His works on our behalf, however, we sing first and foremost because we love Him. Anything short of beginning a service with songs of praise and adoration strips away the hallowed, leaving worship hollow.

Furthermore, praise is essential to healthy, spiritual living. When we are thankful, we feel better than when we are critical. When we are thankful, we are more prone to activate faith, not fear. When we are thankful, we more easily control our thoughts, "casting down strongholds" (2 Corinthians 10:4) and defeating the "prince of the powers of the air" (Ephesians 2:2).

Praise is also a strategic element to overcoming. Praise changes our environment and hence the way in which we view our circumstances. Putting praise on our lips brightens the nature of our perspective. When we override the negativity in our mind, we soon sing our way out of the doldrums and into a more preferable mind-set. Praise invokes the promises of the Lord, once memorized yet momentarily forgotten.

In the heat of hardship, humans leak. Even worship leaders, from time to time, think the grass might be greener in another setting. Wanderlust is a trap. Fatigued by the challenges in one's current setting, worship leaders can be seduced to think that starting afresh will make all that is wrong right. "Wherever you go," one evangelist chided, "there you are!" Relocating during great tumult generally adds to your problems.

Author Elizabeth Elliot elaborates, "The point of life is to see Christ in us, not us in another set of circumstances." Sometimes God allows tests to mold and shape us. Exiting the trial prematurely only suggests a recapitulation later on. Persons in the cauldron need to sing, not run. As we sing, we refill and recall the truths we have learned.

- "I can do all things through Christ who strengthens me" (Philippians 4:13).
- "No weapon formed against us can prosper" (Isaiah 54:17).
- "My God shall supply all our needs" (Philippians 4:19).
- "The Lord will perfect that which concerns me" (Psalm 138:8).
- "Not one word of all of God's promise has failed" (Joshua 21:45).

In other words, praise is an act of spiritual warfare. When the adversary whispers, lies, and attempts to discourage, attending to the opening praise on a Sunday morning with purpose and vigor causes the works of hell to cease and desist. Similarly, when a church grasps the truth that we are servants of the Most High God, privileged to bring honor to His name before asking or apologizing, we authenticate the principle that He is the reason we sing. He is our all-in-all. He is our audience of one.

Musical Skills Are Not as Important as Listening Skills

At first blush, this observation appears paradoxical. Here's what I mean. Musical prowess is a given in terms of a worship leader's qualification. Worship will not rise to the level of moving people to enter in—leaving their pain, sadness, or fear at the front door—unless a worship presentation's beauty encompasses a church like the tentacles of an octopus. Bernard Kelly offers reinforcement, "The apprehension of beauty awakens the deeper, more searching activity of the mind." The aesthetics of worship matter.

However, there is more. Beyond pastoral musicianship, a sensitivity to the mission of the Holy Spirit is essential. Talent clearly unlocks the door, but obedience to the prompting of the Holy Spirit pushes the door wide open! The challenge for young worship leaders is to not rely solely on talent, but instead pursue intimacy. Jesus would say, "My sheep listen to my voice" (John 10:27).

Listening in the prayer closet is a learned behavior. Worship leaders who wait on the Lord in earnest function with understanding in the spirit realm during a presentation. From experience, I contend that waiting begets fullness. Fullness begets intimacy with God. Intimacy begets the prophetic: the refilling, renewing, recovering, and repurposing that weary pilgrims all need. "Burdens are lifted at Calvary,"[8] the old gospel refrain proclaims. However, that kind of granularity—that kind of insight during the leading of worship—comes with a cost. Put simply, we need to stop talking in prayer so He, the Master Musician, can start to talk.

Active listening presupposes a laserlike focus and an acute self-discipline. At worship's core, one's quiet time spawns the retrieval from a worship leader's memory banks of the right song for the right moment. Listening accomplishes a prophetic task that mere planning cannot.

With intentionality, therefore, a worship leader can access God's plan to rescue and redeem hurting persons and thereby minister provision to the congregation while singing. Theologians would call this practice "being dependent upon the Lord." Apart from dependency, one tends to choose more popular or sophomoric songs for worship. Those songs simply fulfill an element of liturgy but lack prophetic power.

By the same token, when a song has been chosen while on bended knee, the Lord rends the sky! A vibrant quiet time with the Lord prepares the heart for receiving impressions from the Lord, provides the patience needed until the directives and creativity come, and proves the promise, "They that wait upon the Lord will renew their strength" (Isaiah 40:31).

This personal time with Jesus is separate from the time necessary to confer with the pastor or rehearse with the worship team. An important

---

[8] "Burdens Are Lifted At Calvary," https://www.jesus-is-savior.com/sounds/Hymns/burdens_are_lifted.htm.

element of the Kingdom with regard to prayer, meditation, and solitude is a peerless weapon in the hand of a balanced worship leader.

> *Being with God is more*
> *important than doing for God.*
>
> *—Dr. Earl D. Baldwin*[8]

There is an important distinction here. The worship leader must, of necessity, learn the voice of the Shepherd in order to keep the sheep on the right path. Showmanship won't cut it. Being cute won't satisfy. Only walking with Jesus privately prepares a worship leader to flow in the Spirit publicly. There is no other way in which to mature as a Christian other than to adopt active listening skills in prayer.

> *Mark Twain once quipped, "The*
> *difference between the almost right*
> *word and the right word is the*
> *difference between the lightning*
> *bug and the lightning!" The same*
> *is true with song selection.*

Author Stephen Covey remarks, "Most people do not listen with the intent to understand; they listen with the intent to reply." In the work of the Kingdom, listening is life-giving. Until we perceive the intent of the Spirit for any given Sunday, we cannot possibly choose the right songs for the journey into His presence beforehand.

Worship, Although Sung, Is Not a Concert

Avoiding the fad to concertize worship is the great challenge of the contemporary church. We have evolved the art of worship into its own tower of Babel. Too often we have maximized the show and left an intimacy with Jesus in the dust. Our new platforms feature "shock and awe." Amid the cacophony, how can one possibly hear the "still, small voice"?

Interestingly the same sophisticated evolution happened in classical music. Bach's counterpoint gave rise to Mozart's manicured orchestration. Beethoven's bluster gave rise to Braham's moodiness. Tchaikovsky's

---

[9] From a sermon by Dr. Earl D. Baldwin, preached at Trinity Life Church, Baltimore, MD

melodies gave rise to Rachmaninoff's melancholy. Then Stravinsky just brilliantly blew the stage up with *The Rite of Spring*. Today's classical composers write what is, to the average concertgoer, barely understandable if appreciated at all.

The great mishap in business, according to guru Tom Peters, is that management frequently "promotes employees to their maximum level of inefficiency." I am disquieted by the reality that worship in many settings is programmed exclusively for one generation over another. Those who are stylistically ignored are left to sit and stew, bored and disenfranchised. How inefficient! Yet our Lord was inclusive of all the cultures and generations of His time.

In Matthew 9:36, we read, "When He saw the crowds He had compassion on them, because they were harassed and helpless, like sheep without a shepherd." Matthew Henry notes, "Jesus visited not only the great and wealthy cities but the poor, obscure villages and there preached." Our Lord went everywhere and spoke to everyone. He left no one out.

Since musical preferences for each generation present are unique to the taste of that age group, shouldn't we plan ahead to offer something prized by each generation as often as possible? Should we leave anyone out? In most churches, up to four generations currently attend services by virtue of medical advances. I wonder if those older generations, excluded week after week from singing anything with which they relate, feel like sheep without a shepherd? I think we can do better!

The human spirit was created to inquire, to research, and to invent. In medicine, for example, a quest for the cure is essential. In technology, research and development teams have transformed the way in which we communicate. These are good things. In the music of worship, one longs for the perfect moment when lyric and melody, harmonic structure, and rhythmic feel find their equilibrium. When they do, amid rarified air, all the world stands still. All our pain subsides, and all we feel is Jesus in the room!

The songwriter of another time and place said it this way, "It will be worth it all when we see Jesus. Life's trials will seem so small when we see Christ. One glimpse of His dear face all sorrows will erase. So bravely run the race 'till we see Christ."

All sorrows will erase! It is in that moment of exchange—trials for a glimpse and ashes for beauty—that the elusive quality of still, not the bombastically complex, ministers to the lost, the disabled, the hurting, and the dying. In other words, if the tempo is right, the groove is in the pocket, and the band members know how to improvise discerningly, one may achieve transcendence. That is what Bernard Kelly meant. In a moment of sheer beauty, the mind is free to embrace the Divine. Perhaps that is why Robert Shaw, the preeminent American choral conductor, referred to sacred music as "almost sacramental." When the feel of the song is tasteful, the people can bask in His presence.

Keeping the musical element of a worship encounter pure is harder than it sounds. Poets ache to find the simple, the elegant, and the perfect phrase. Sculptors sweat to mold clay for days removing excess. Editing worship until one finds the essence, the authentic expression of what the Lord is saying is a beguiling task. Guarding a congregation from distractions, in the final analysis, is the work of an artist. It is far easier just to make things too busy, too loud for too long. Yet as the Word said in utter simplicity, "Be still and know that I am God" (Psalm 46:10).

> *Stillness, like silence, is priceless.*

God Commits to Character, Not Talent[10]

A pastoral musician cannot possibly present the songs of the church with excellence unless the music is accompanied by a complimentary skill set. These skills include making prayer a daily activity, having each other's back, and guarding the tongue. Clearly all staff members must manage ministerial details with precision. Yet equally important is the ability to care for people's health and well-being with the precision of a surgeon.

At worship's core, leading is first and foremost about following Jesus in the little things, such as "loving the unlovely" (Matthew 8:1–5) or giving "a cup of cold water to a weary passerby" (Matthew 10:42). Finding your equilibrium as a worship leader involves a trifecta of musicianship, people skills, and spirituality.

Spiritual formation is often underplayed in the development of a fully orbed worship leader. A leader's spiritual awareness has many facets.

---

[10] From a conversation I had with author Edwin Louis Cole.

Some are related to time management. For example, being sensitive to the interruptions that momentarily take a worship leader off task are small sacrifices that carry weight in the Kingdom.

Interruptions matter! The cell rings; someone needs counsel. There's a knock at the door; someone needs prayer. People get sick; tragedy suddenly invades a home. People lose jobs; bills pile up. There are times in which the worship leader needs to offer compassion before the daily checklist is completed. This understanding reflects an emotional intelligence, or EQ. Educational psychologists define emotional intelligence as the capacity to not only perceive and internalize data correctly but to also relate well to diverse groups of people. This ability reflects interpersonal skill. Jesus often chose people over tasks. The wise worship leader is good at both.

It has been said that talent is doing easily what others find difficult. However, talent is never enough! God commits to character. This remark is all about the rest of the iceberg—unseen to the naked eye. From a ship's point of view, the visible part of an iceberg is relatively small. Just ask the captain of the *Titanic*! Underneath the frigid water, the iceberg is huge.

God is committed to blessing what people cannot see. The Almighty cares about the heart of a leader. What is considered inside a leader's mind affects what occurs outside in ministry behavior and decision-making. Ultimately the heart affects everything a leader aspires to accomplish. If the heart is pure, the ministry will advance in healthy ways. If the heart is flawed, problems quickly ensue. Said another way, "Man looks at the appearance, but God looks at the heart" (1 Samuel 16:7).

Keeping the heart soft amid the many tests, trials, and temptations of life is demanding to be sure. Tests are hard won. Often trials are lengthy, and temptations can burn like wildfire. So when the scripture says "endure hardship," my eyes open widely. Enduring hardships successfully means we strive to avoid bitterness; forgive quickly when falsely accused or betrayed; avoid spreading gossip when hurt; rigorously confront the adversary in prayer; contend for revival when there are no visible signs of progress; never, ever give up on your call; and manage church politics the right way when thrown under the bus.

Reacting to heartbreaking setbacks with spiritual fortitude is a worthy goal. Still the wounds of a friend have a way of lingering. They take time to work out. After a while, scars mount, and in retrospect, most humans develop regrets. Pastor Joel Osteen elaborates, "One can be a product of your past, but you don't have to be a prisoner to your past."

I have firsthand experience with being wounded in ministry. I know the anguish of harboring ill against a colleague. I know the bite of withholding forgiveness. The feeling of being thrashed by a trusted friend's betrayal is unspeakably demoralizing. It has been said of anger, "Being angry is like drinking poison and expecting the person with whom you are angry to die. The problem is that you drank the poison!" The same fate is attributed to those who somehow are unwilling to forgive.

> *The prolific writer, C. S. Lewis, aptly observed, "To be a Christian means to forgive the inexcusable because God has forgiven the inexcusable in you."*

Forgiveness is not a condoning of the perpetrator's actions. Forgiveness is an act of liberation that sets you and me free from the haunting memories. Forgiveness, by God's design, soothes the soul. It removes the sting by letting it go. Forgiveness essentially gives the matter to God. This is critically important. Luke writes, "It is impossible that wounds won't come" (17:1).

Ministerial points of tension are merely grounds for altar building. The tests we pass, choosing the way of the cross over the way of vengeance, sets us up for great reward in the Kingdom. Jesus said, "Forgive them for they know not what they do" (Luke 23:34). Saying those words aloud have helped me forgive the friends who betrayed. After all, unforgiveness leads to bitterness. Becoming a bitter individual is not worth it. Someone once said the difference between *bitter* and *better* was the letter "I." We have a choice.

Paul affirms, "Do not be overcome by evil but overcome evil with good" (Romans 12:21). I choose God's way. I am determined to live life proactively. Place your former colleagues and enemies in God's hands. Forgive, move forward, don't look back like Lot's wife, and live a great life. If I can, you can too!

One more thing: I take great comfort from the fact that tragic acts of nature only last for a season. A large fire eventually burns out. Hurricanes come and go. The storm passes by. So it is with interpersonal pain in a ministry context. "And it came to pass ... " This phrase is dotted throughout the Bible. Beyond being a transitional phrase, it has meaning on its own!

People wound. The adversary taunts. We grieve momentarily, but Jesus won the day on Calvary. He said, "It is finished!" The devil, who always augments pain and suffering in the night, knows his future. We simply have to remind him of it occasionally, which is only accomplished through obedience to the Word and contending in the prayer closet.

Noted author E. M. Bounds punctuates, "The work of the ministry is prayer."

Building Trust

Here are five ways in which to build trust.

1. Spend time together.
2. Work through disagreement together.
3. Acknowledge conflicts are inevitable.
4. Realize hell plots to divide the staff through subterfuge and jealousy.
5. Be aware discipline and duplicity are the opposite sides of the same coin.

Spend time together, period! Author Gary Chapman, in his landmark book *The Five Love Languages*, cited a valuable criterion in the building of a healthy relationship, "Quality time." If a church is going to thrive, one must have time alone with the pastor on a regular basis. There is no substitute for this meeting. Jesus spent time with the Father. He prayed in earnest. He was honest and transparent. Upon knowing the Father's heart, He was obedient.

The greatest cause for misunderstanding and the eventual termination of a worship leader is a bothersome uncertainty that slowly begins to grow in the pastor's heart. This uncertainty stems from assumptions the pastor makes about a worship leader's motivations, mistakes, or mismanagement. This uneasiness thrives in an atmosphere in which quality time is absent.

Insecurity fuels this uncertainty. How ironic that pastors who succumb to insecurity often become unwitting co-conspirators in the plots of hell to destroy the very church they serve. If there is a kink in the armor of a leader, the adversary will take full advantage. His game plan is to whisper confusion, agitate, and sow thoughts of dissembling, enmity, and strife. The adversary will create subplots and subterfuge until the leader broods at night—counting his fears rather than counseling his faith. The bottom line is if there is no unity between the pastor and the worship leader, how will there be an anointing in the Sunday service?

From my point of view, another reason for pastoral mistrust is jealousy. Pure and simple! At times, a worship leader can be winsome. The right song for the right corporate moment wins the respect of the people. If the worship leader is gregarious in addition to choosing worship material with apt perceptibility, the fondness of the congregation grows deeper.

I am reminded of the incendiary words the children of Israel chanted in the time of King Saul. "Saul has slain his thousands but David his tens of thousands" (1 Samuel 18:7). Unfortunately I have seen this scenario repeated many times. A pastor hires a gifted musician. The musician does well while the pastor grows resentful. Things usually end poorly for the musician.

From day one, as a young worship leader, I would press for weekly coffee with the pastor. I would entreat his friendship with questions and advice, wisdom, and counsel. I would further advocate a weekly time of prayer. At all cost I would be loyal, for I believe it to be impossible to grow a church without first developing a healthy working relationship with the pastor.

> *Popular speaker Beth Moore says, "Slander represents a pride and arrogance in the person who talks in this manner. And if slander is allowed, the blessings of the Lord in our lives are hindered."*

Friendship can bond a missional mind-set in both pastor and worship leader if time together is prioritized. Without healthy communication though, trust may never fully materialize—much less cement the two ministers against the adversary's flood of contention. If there are kinks in the armor of a pastoral team, be assured subterfuge, like a weed in a garden, will pierce through. If that gossip is not crushed early on, cooperation devolves into competition.

Perhaps that is why Paul admonishes us to "think on things of a good report" (Philippians 4:8), squelching the adversary's bitter root.

Work through disagreement together. In Luke, we read, "It is impossible that offenses won't come" (Luke 17:1). Two like-minded pastoral leaders who come together to build a house of prayer bring with them not only a skill set but growing edges that are not fully formed. The skills that work well between both leaders are called competencies. Their heart for ministry and their devotion to Christ in personal life choices are called character traits.

However, the way in which both leaders work through each other's growing edges is called chemistry. If a leader likes another, he or she will give the benefit of the doubt when skirmishes arise. If, however, the leader somehow does not appreciate aspects of the other's personality, he or she may be more likely to terminate.

The critical element in a pastoral relationship that stands the tests of time—the stuff of longevity—is directly related to the affinity that exists between the church pastor and the worship leader. In short, one has to like the person with whom he or she is working. If there is an admiration, shared interests, humor, and mutuality, the hard times will be palatable. Otherwise, the lack of Christlikeness will cause the boat to lose its rudder.

Of this, I know firsthand. Beware of the interview that concludes without the sparks of a potential new friend. Trust me.

Conflicts are inevitable. The church is a hospital. Healing the sick is messy. Sometimes emergencies are uncomfortable, inconvenient, and life-threatening. Even our Lord couldn't avoid conflict. He and Peter argued. Judas betrayed. The Pharisees taunted, and often Jesus was rejected. Consider those verbs: argue, betray, taunt, and reject. They do not sound inviting, do they?

The difference between an argument and a debate is noteworthy. A debate is impersonal, a passionate advocating of an idea or core value. An argument, by contrast, turns personal. The way to win an argument is to come back to your accuser in the opposite spirit. When a colleague or leader speaks arrogantly or with temper, respond softly. Don't bite back.

Apply this axiom: He who guards his tongue in a moment of anger saves himself a hundred days of pain.

Managing your spirit amid another's outburst of anger is perilous. These clashes create painful wounds. They imply a close relationship has been torn apart. Any relationship that suffers treachery will not heal quickly. Heart issues are at stake and will only be repaired with the help of the Holy Spirit. Jesus tried to help Judas, but the former treasurer was bound and determined.

At some dimension, we are all broken. We have all suffered rejection. The New Testament is full of examples of taking that kind of pain in stride.

> *Better by far to work out our pain with Jesus. He knows the feelings of our infirmity. He knows how to keep confidences.*

I know it is not easy, but our security is in Him. Attacks will come. When they do, the way of the Lord is to "count it all joy" (James 1:2). It is important in ministry when assaulted by the darts of the evil one, not to take matters into our own hands. Often we make a mess out of responding to rejection through bitterness or any other tactic of self-preservation.

Hell plots to divide the staff through subterfuge and jealousy. Building a church is not for the faint of heart, especially if you are effective in front of people. Others may soon covet your poise. The immature among us will compare their lack to your plenty. This is human nature. During my parish ministry, I tried to live out one particular definition of leadership at all times: "Leadership is an elegance of conduct."

Interestingly there are no caveats to that characterization. This description does not imply leaders should be elegant only when the sun is shining or applicable only on the day of a promotion. Leadership is elegant at all times in the heat of battle, when oppressed by an adversary or even

> *"As for me and my worship team, we will serve the Lord!"*
>
> —*Joshua 24:15, paraphrase*

a jealous friend, amid great loss, when denied credit for a winning idea, when lied to, when yelled at, and when cursed and thrown away.

Many books on leadership

remark extensively about how to rebound after a significant loss. Inventors never quit; nor do visionaries. Will you?

Discipline and duplicity are the opposite sides of the same coin. Further I am aware that pastors and worship leaders are oftentimes polar opposites in the way in which their brains function, where their interests lay, and how their management styles differ. Most pastors I know are decisive. Most worship leaders are dreamy. Many pastors are organized and prompt. Many worship leaders are spontaneous and lots of fun. The differences could go on for days.

What is important is not a binary conclusion, such as, pastors are professional and worship leaders are scattered. What is important is that opposites attract, and they have to work carefully with each other in the fulfillment of God's design for the church. Differences in personality, learning style, time management, and a host of other data points pale in

> *The administrative and artistic temperament need to understand each other's viewpoint and thereby work through ministry objectives in positive ways.*

comparison to the valuable, complementary way in which different gift mixes can successfully collaborate in the implementation of a worship experience for the church.

Harshly disciplining a worship leader for his or her learning style may be like killing a fly with a bazooka. Moreover, having a worship leader who comes from a legalistic background criticize a pastor's weekday attire when the pastor comes from a more casual background is petty.

This is why I am so fervent about working with colleagues who have chemistry, not merely credentials. I am also passionate about the need for regular, honest, and open communication. Before one disciplines a subordinate, learn about his or her background, taste, dreams, and administrative style.

> *Discipline and duplicity are the opposite sides of the same coin. In the ministry, they can be overplayed, falsely assumed, and used to hammer a common misunderstanding.*

Before a subordinate creates subterfuge by finding fault with what is thought of as a matter of duplicity in their leader, the worship leader needs to know how a pastor thinks about his or her place in the community, thoughts on making others feel comfortable in his or her presence, and what his or her personal evangelism strategy affects his or her daily choices.

I opened this chapter juxtaposing *hallowed* with *hollow worship*. Often the way we treat each other during the workweek plays into whether the Lord's presence manifests on Sunday. God is just. He sees all we do. He cares about the little foxes in our lives. Be circumspect, dear worship leader. Don't judge so quickly. Put the needs of others ahead of your own. Be a prayerful leader for prayerlessness leads to carelessness.

The eminent devotional writer, Oswald Chambers, concludes, "If we do not purposely sacrifice the natural, the supernatural can never be natural to us." As a worship leader, there are certain things I cannot afford. Among them are the dark sides of human nature (anger, backbiting, and getting even) and a pervasive professional sloppiness (procrastination, fudging the truth, and avoiding the spiritual practices).

Removing the dross in our lives is hard-won but necessary because these unfortunate habits dull the working of the Spirit. Candidly, it is the supernatural among us that distinguishes *hallowed* from mere *hollow* in public worship expressions.

Seeds from the Core

1. The relationship between a pastor and worship leader is fragile. Handle it with care.
2. A vibrant devotional life is essential in becoming the best worship leader you can possibly be.
3. Interpersonal skills are invaluable in the work of ministry.
4. Hallowed worship stimulates; hollow worship simulates.

To achieve great things, two things are needed:
A plan and not quite enough time!

—Leonard Bernstein

CHAPTER 6

IT'S TIME TO SING

In May 2016, the director of Arts Education for the Los Angeles Unified School District invited me to become a choral teacher at a historic downtown high school. In August, I began to teach music to bilingual Latino students in East LA. The challenges were multifaceted.

For example, there had not been a full-time choral conductor at the school for over two decades. There was no significant feeder system in place. There was no sense of a choral culture at the school. Practically all my students had never even sung in a choir before. I was literally starting from scratch.

To make matters worse, the choir was divided into three classes. We would rarely rehearse as a unit. The classes were filled with students who ranged from gifted to problematic and from highly motivated to those with no interest in singing at all. Frankly, most students had requested guitar or piano class but were placed into the choir because the other classes were full.

Let me triangulate this dilemma succinctly: a new teacher, a large group of disappointed students, and a choral opportunity in which most students had little, if any, interest. It took me a month to win the argument that it is not enough in life to simply attend class. To succeed, one has to pay attention and actually try! Then there was the challenge of motivating my students to take a deep breath, sing in tune, and open one's mouth wide enough in order to purify a vowel or voice a consonant. I was stuck. I needed a miracle.

Have you ever been in a situation that was so dark, from a human point of view, that you could see no way out except for a supernatural intervention? Eight weeks into the semester, my middle choral class was suddenly interrupted with a loud knock on the rehearsal hall door. A student answered. I was summoned to the door with a question from a guidance counselor, "Dr. McDonald, would you please accept this new student from Guatemala?"

Now the middle of my three sections of choir students was unique. To begin, 30 percent of this class contained students who only spoke a few words of English. I strategically placed student interpreters amid clusters of these students so we could communicate. The guys of the class were a rough combination of well-behaved and discipline-prone. The addition of one new young man could throw the balance of behavior if I were not judicious.

So I quickly requested a translator and inquired of the prospective new student,

- Do you know how to sing? *Yes.*
- Do you like to sing? *Very much.*
- Can you play an instrument? *Yes.*
- How many? *I can play five instruments!*
- Would you sing a solo for us? *Oh yes.*

Without knowing David at all, I brought him to the grand piano facing the students in the front of the hall and introduced him. For some reason, I had asked the final question spontaneously. Because of his enthusiasm, I decided on the spot to experiment. What happened next will forever be emblazoned on my memory. There in my music studio, amid a student body foreign to the power of a song, an angel showed up dressed as a young teenager from another country.

David took a breath! He threw his shoulders back, and he sang for all he was worth—full voice, dramatic, confident, and self-assured. Tears immediately filled my eyes. The young ladies swooned. The well-behaved young men found a hero. The discipline-prone found a vanguard. The milieu of my class was transformed in the blink of an eye! Suddenly the class had passion and purpose.

A week later, two more musical teens joined the class as well, emanating from the same knock on the door. As I write this chapter, we are days from singing a Christmas concert where these Hispanic exemplars, my three miracle students from heaven, will sing in perfect harmony supporting my burgeoning high school choir. After they sing, I'll pause on that secular stage to whisper a prayer.

David's unexpected entrance that October afternoon affirmed that Jesus truly cares. He cared enough to enter my world in the exact way I needed. He cared enough to send a teenage boy to awaken the value of a song in my students. He cared enough to use something seemingly weak and vulnerable to confound the cool among us.

The lessons from this "miracle gift" are important. They have implications and applications for all worship leaders internationally.

Implications

Jesus cares about His worship leaders no matter what profession they practice. Jesus loves music! He often rides on the wings of a song to transform everything about our lives and the lives of our constituencies. Jesus cares about the disenfranchised around us. He is not limited by our structures or predispositions. When a believer prays, angels are quickly dispersed! Jesus is still in the miracle business. No matter how dark your situation is, He is "as close as the mention of His name."[11]

Applications

Jesus summoned Philip to witness to a politician in the desert. No environment is too far off the beaten path for a miracle provision from the Lord. Although I live in a world-class city, at this moment, I am teaching in one of the at-risk communities of urban LA. Nevertheless, on the day of my visitation, Jesus

> *Your locale is not the issue;*
> *the prayerful invitation*
> *of His Presence is!*

came in power and authority, answering my plea, solving my problem, and setting the captives in my classroom free. He'll do the same for you!

---

[11] Gordon Jensen, "He's as Close as the Mention of His Name," 1978.

The value the godhead places on music in the scriptures is legendary. On the night that Jesus was born, angels sang. In the prison cell, Paul and Silas sang. The prophet in 2 Kings, frustrated by the poor judgment of the kings, uttered, "Now bring me a musician!" Resultantly, impartation came, and the enemy was soundly defeated.

Singing, my friend, is never casual with the Lord. Singing evokes His presence. Songs rally the people. Songs vanquish the adversary's advance. Some in my past tried to instill into my burgeoning theology that singing was simply a preliminary to the event of the day, the Sunday sermon. But my walk with Jesus has borne irrefutable data to the contrary. I have seen a song invoke healing grace. I've witnessed songs in worship settings soften hardened hearts, woo nonbelievers, and foster forgiveness in families.

Father God sent music to the world as a gift for all. Some say music is the international language. All can relate. All can appreciate. All can find peace, hope, and love afresh as songs are sung. Those are secular understandings mutually shared among all the people of the earth. Musicologists and music educators all agree on the inherent power embedded in a song.

> *Songs don't necessarily need a sermon, but a sermon always needs a song!*

But there is more. Songs presented under the anointing wage war in the spirit realm. They move beyond the natural into the supernatural. From the pages of Scripture, we note that music is an undeniable force in heaven itself. When we pray, God will often answer with a song "in the night season."

Worship leaders, take heart! Our God is all-knowing. He multitasks on a global scale. Nothing escapes His logic or, more importantly, His love. He sent Jesus into a lowly manger paradoxically amid thunderous praise in the form of choral singing. I take great joy in that juxtaposition. Just think as a manager and a heavenly choir! He can inspire you in your humble place of ministry. He will inform your decisions with just the right song for breakthrough. He

> *Don't give up! Don't give in! It seems to me that Bethlehem moments are His specialty.*

will send angels to minister, protect, and transform your setting, just as

He did for me the day David came to my humble, fifth-period choir rehearsal.

Pastor Bill Johnson reflects, "Impossibilities will bend their knee to the name of Jesus. May His love bring breakthrough to you today!" I stand in agreement. Grace is just around your corner. Stories like my encounter with an unexpected angel in my classroom are important to share. The Holy Bible supports this assertion, stating, "They overcame by the blood of the Lamb and the word of their testimony" (Revelation 12:11). Sharing the miraculous stories of our lives not only edify us but bring hope to others who may be facing similar challenges. How I wish you could meet the miracle men of my first year of teaching.

There, David, Alex, and Joselino brought a fresh revelation of God's grace to my weary heart. There, a miracle occurred to rally my troops. There, I found that Jesus really cares.

There, your relationship with our Lord can be as real and potent as mine. Joel Osteen has aptly noted, "Your prayers open the door for Him to move in your life. Keep standing! Keep believing! Keep praying—knowing that He is working behind the scenes and orchestrating things in your favor."

Knowing how much music means to our Lord, it is fitting that the story of my classroom miracle serves as an advanced organizer for the topic at hand. Friends, it's time to sing! This chapter is all about the elements of a song in a worship context. We will discuss how to choose a song and how to effectively teach a song to the church you serve. We will also discuss just how to create a flow of worship that bows before majesty and ennobles the wounded heart. We will conclude this chapter discussing how to structure a medley of songs that will lead worshippers to the God moment in a worship encounter.

How to Choose a Song

Not all songs are germane to the worship encounter. Some songs are written for one's personal devotions. Enough said. Others are meant to be inspirational. They are written for a trained singer and slightly above the heads of the normal congregant's musical capacity. Still, other songs are compositionally incomplete. They were written without enough attention to detail. They may contain a sophomoric lyric or a melody that does not rise to the appropriate level of musical mystery. You see, poetry and melodic

> *Choosing the right song, therefore, presupposes careful analysis and active listening skills.*

composition seem easy to perform but are deceptively difficult to create. It is important for the musical shepherd of the church to protect the sheep from the awkward, the poorly written, and the mediocre.

Regarding the Lyrics

When choosing a song, one must carefully analyze just what your church will sing. Songs, from the perspective of a church community, become paragraphs in a love letter the congregation literally reads (sings) to the Master. I begin from the element that is most important to the congregation, the words of the song.

Throughout the course of my ministry, slogans within the body of Christ have been effective ways for me to remember what is important about Christianity. For purposes of definition, I have chosen to elaborate four slogans. These sayings frame the rubric by which I filter a new song's lyrical potential.

Jesus Is My All-in-All

One of the greatest errors new worship leaders make is to essentially choose songs that are on their playlist, are popular in social media, are somehow trendy to sing, or are generationally exclusive.

Rather than choosing songs merely because they are popular, I affirm choosing songs for worship that speak about our Lord Jesus. If we worship Him as the paramount theme of our worship, we in effect lift Him high. The Bible confirms, "If I be lifted up, I will draw all men unto me" (John 12:3).

Save the trendy for a youth encounter. Save the testimony songs for an offertory. Save your favorite songs by your favorite artist for your personal devotional time or your commute.

When choosing songs for a multigenerational, severely tested, sin-prone, faith-leaking congregation, sing loudly about the attributes of Jesus. Worship His majesty. Honor His unshakable love for us. Remember His sacrifice. Bless His holy name. Focusing on Him is enough. He is our glorious Redeemer. Mentioning His works invokes His presence. If His presence comes to dwell among us, everything of a generational bias will melt away along with our burdens, fears, and past failures.

Something Good Is Going to Happen to You

This slogan became a mantra of Oral Roberts, a prominent healing evangelist in the twentieth century. His meetings, TV specials, and university all attested to the goodness of the Lord. Consequently, growing up in the States, I found peace in His message, joy in His optimism, and grace in His belief that healing is a part of the Christian walk.

Something good referred to the fact that regardless of our circumstances, God is able. God is good. That unquenchable optimism in the face of gloom is what the church is all about. Jesus came into the world to make a difference. The gospel is noteworthy. Just to catch a glimpse of its power by listening to an anointed worship refrain in the middle of an individual's pressing challenge is suddenly finding water in the desert.

With that being said, I told my seminary students all the time to look tirelessly for songs with hope-filled lyrical content. The research required to locate new songs that declare God's ability to heal, to countermand the plots of the evil one, and to break through with life-changing relief are priceless to a weary-worn congregant.

Life is hard, but Jesus is ever true. We can never lose sight of our mission, our purpose, and His passion. I believe something good is going to happen to you!

Already and Not Yet

There is something mystical about the concept of faith. Faith hopes. Faith contends. Faith never gives up. Occasionally, for our own growth and development, faith is also tested. In the middle of a test of faith like an illness, setback, or betrayal, it is crucial to sing faith-based songs when a church family convenes.

Songs steady us in moments of confusion. They comfort us in moments of dismay. I will always remember the gospel song that was written during my first church assignment, "When Answers Aren't Enough." That song (Google the lyrics) always brought me "peace in the midst of the storm."[12]

Let's be honest. Believers tend to leak God's promises amid the times of "enduring hardship" (2 Timothy 4:5). They need weekly support from the songs of worship in order to wage the war that sudden attacks and hurtful wounds produce. From personal, anecdotal evidence, I know how hard it is to say good-bye to a loved one. Without grace, it is nearly impossible to forgive an enemy or understand the purpose of a wild tragedy like a home invasion. Yet from my point of view, having led worship for forty years, I can also speak to the redemptive quality that unified singing in church provides when we are under attack.

We all want to say along with the apostle Paul, "I know how to abound and to be debased" (Philippians 4:12). Abounding is the easy part. Being debased is the challenge But there is a remedy. Singing, you see, can help us deflect the embarrassment of a loss- of- face, so often experienced during a debasing trial. Songs help to anesthetize shock. Songs remind us that we already have a measure of faith, yet as long as we live on this fallen planet, we may not perceive the complete picture of why things occurred as they did.

So we sing, and while we are singing, we are filled again with His grace for a time. That empowerment helps us to trust amid the fire, to be content amid the loss. So we sing on Sunday in church. More importantly, we also sing "in the night season." Choosing night songs is a core value of a maturing worship leader (Job 35:10). In times of anxiety, congregants will need

> *Night songs then remind us of the divine paradox: Already but not yet.*

the vocabulary that only a night song offers. Internalizing a night song's lyric informs our emotional behavior in trial … sometimes.

This is what the third slogan is all about. When all that we know is taken away, Christians throughout the annals of time have come to grips with their belief system by quoting the phrase, "Already and not yet." We

---

[12] Scott Wesley Brown, "When Answers Aren't Enough," 2005.

know God is real, but until heaven is finalized, we won't know fully how wonderful He was.

Suddenly I Was in the Spirit

John on the Isle of Patmos, while writing the last book of the Bible, Revelation, often remarked that as he was waiting on the Lord, "Suddenly, [he] was in the Spirit" (Revelation 1:10). All worship leaders need spiritual understanding when choosing songs that the church will sing in the future.

From my experience, the songs that really connected and stood the test of time were the ones that moved the people beyond their current circumstance into the very presence of God. So naturally, that phrase haunted me in times of song selection. How could I be sure that the song I was drawn to would transform the room and engage the people to worship? I remember feeling the weight of my decision, my choice.

Instinctively, I understand that some songs merely entertained, while only a precious few actually brought the anointing into the sanctuary. Differentiating between the two reference points, however, when selecting a new song was a challenge. I would learn from experience that anointed songs always captivate the congregant not to measure the size of their problem, but the size of Jesus's ability to heal, to restore, and to obliterate the works of darkness. Amid the singing of an anointed song, congregants are healed, retooled, and forgiven.

As I grew to practice the presence of the Lord in my private devotions, I became more assured of His desire to guide my worship repertoire selections. Active listening when in the prayer closet is worth all the effort of sitting at His feet, learning His ways, and waiting on Him. In short, when I was before the Lord in

> *Suddenly, John wrote, I was in the spirit, but that suddenly for me took years to master.*

prayerful analysis of a song's lyrical worth, I chose not to exclusively favor the glib or popular ballad; instead I chose the song that edified the Lord and focused a congregation on His matchless ability to create a sudden breakthrough.

Regarding the Melody

What makes a worship song great? What are the elements of a musical composition that mysteriously coalesce to grab the attention of millennials, boomers, and seniors? The question of greatness with regard to artistic composition is one that has baffled composers, performers, and music professors alike. For most people, greatness is easy to recognize but difficult to define.

Consider Beethoven's *Fifth Symphony*, Rachmaninoff's *Second Piano Concerto*, and Rutter's *Candlelight Carol*. The great works of art are all alike in this manner. Their inherent beauty defies generational lines, contemporary fads, and the trends of any time. Artistic greatness is oblivious to custom and culture. Great songs speak to all of us in a timeless fashion. More specifically, a great song has an inspired melody, which readily soothes the listener. A great song also has a compositional form that combines useful repetition with an occasional surprise. A great song always has something that defies mere logic and transforms our perspective.

So choose worship songs carefully. The right song at the right moment makes our days sweet and our failures forgivable. Be a wise shepherd. Guard against "the prowler" of mediocre composition. Beware "the pitfall" of the testimony song, the one that elevates man's cleverness as opposed to God's worthiness. Ignore the temptation to capitulate to what is popular with only your generation. Your responsibility extends not only to include the tastes of the two generations ahead of you, but the one growing up behind you as well.

One more thing: By choosing generationally inclusive repertoire, we help to ensure that the words of the new song are not uniformly dismissed because of a trendy melody or harmonic structure that people from other generations simply don't relate to. In the final analysis, a congregation cannot afford the luxury of only singing the songs they like (for aesthetic reasons) when in a trial-by-fire. When the heat is on, we all need the strength that only a unified singing church musters. Spiritual power is transmitted as we participate, not as we fold our arms in prideful disgust.

The songs you choose comprise the vocabulary your church will articulate in all the seasons of their life. They will sing the songs you choose when facing surgery, important exams, and fiery temptations. These are the songs they will sing on the day they marry and on the day they bury.

How to Teach a New Song

There are five criteria that must be internalized in order to teach a new song effectively.

Master the Song

There is no adequate substitute for personal preparation in the work of the ministry. As a worship leader, if you are not prepared for rehearsal, Sunday's presentation, or in your personal life, the saints may lose heart. That is a distraction. We have a responsibility to care for the people for whom we serve. Preparation is the way we show our congregation they are loved and valued by our Savior. Moreover, when we are on our game, the congregation will feel safe enough to risk being open and vulnerable in God's presence as we lead the weekly worship encounter.

A wise shepherd is always vigilant. Being vigilant means you will always have the right materials in place for a ministry opportunity, rehearsal, or service. Your repertoire will have been thoroughly vetted with the pastor because it is never appropriate to surprise a senior minister in public. Your singers and players will always be prepared when the saints gather to minister to the Lord. As a master musician, you will know the new song well enough to sing it through several times, never deviating from the correct rhythm, melody, or "feel" of the song.

Maintain a Professional Decorum

In this matter, I take a cue from the profession of television journalism. You will notice on TV, the evening newscasters always look polished, never let you know how bad their private life may be, always smile on camera, and read their script flawlessly.

Because you and I are representing the Lord Jesus as we sing, the congregation has a right to expect we will be as organized, systematic, and professional as the TV journalists are. If we are disheveled in appearance, mentally preoccupied, or musically unprepared, how can we expect the faithful to close their eyes and place their cares in the hands of the Lord?

Remove All Distractions

Distractions in the worship arena come in many sizes and shapes. For example, some distractions are self-inflicted by a worship leader who is disorganized. Other distractions occur because of operational error with the technology, be it an electronic keyboard, the PA system, or a computer used to project lyrics on a screen. Still, others are the result of spiritual attack. Always remember, the adversary doesn't want the worship of the church to flow smoothly.

One cannot overemphasize the practical need to test equipment routinely. Furthermore, I believe the worship team should include the media team in times of prayer and vision casting. All worship volunteers must not only practice music but the presence of God as well. Worship times for the larger team are mandatory both for edification and spiritual warfare. If we don't contend together apart from Sunday, we are setting ourselves up for a surprise attack.

Facilitate the Learning Process

The way people learn a song is complex. Many congregants do not read music, so their primary mode of acquiring the melody of a new song is by rote through the ear gate. It is fundamentally important that the song being introduced be sung with rigorous consistency. If the worship leader vacillates in presenting the elements of the song, the congregation will learn the song incorrectly. Changing bad habits after learning a song erroneously are both frustrating and aggravating.

Say Just Enough

The phrase "economy of gesture" is a term often used in college conducting courses to signal the responsibility of a conductor to present orchestral or choral music in a dignified or refined manner. A conductor should avoid being overly dramatic or glitzy. Rather the role of a conductor is to provide direction to the musicians without necessarily grabbing the spotlight.

Interestingly, the same is true for a worship leader. I affirm the notion that in public, musicians should keep directions succinct. When introducing a new song or giving a congregation a word of exhortation, be plainspoken and brief. Avoid at all cost the temptation to preach. That is the pastor's role. Long-windedness is out of vogue!

> *Those who know how to listen to the gentle guidance of the Holy Spirit will choose songs that matter, not mutter.*

These behaviors, fiercely cultivated, will foster trust not only in your musical ability but in your spiritual attentiveness as well.

How to Plan a Flow of Worship

Many years ago, I read a catalytic article on leading worship by Tom Brooks of Hosanna Integrity notoriety. In the article, Tom listed a four-point model for presenting worship that has borne the test of time. For our purposes, it bears recapitulation.

The Brooks Model

1. Choose songs that flow together lyrically.
2. Choose songs that flow together musically.
3. Never repeat last week's worship listing, for it is day-old manna!
4. Don't be afraid to linger in God's presence.

The straightforwardness of the Brooks model is worthy of commentary. Undeniably, one of the most significant proficiencies that worship leaders need is a knack for finding a winning song from the fifty or more that are available to you any given weekday afternoon.

However, once you have found the tune that matters—the rare gem that blesses the soul—there is a second but equally relevant proficiency to master, that of putting the new song amid equally anointed others by which the people who sing the medley on the Lord's day can somehow move beyond their pain and their pride into the very presence of a living God.

Turning sacred songs into a flow of worship is no small task.

Countless Variables Come into Play

- **The weather:** During the rainy season in LA, persons prefer to stay home. If they do travel out on a Sunday, they are generally late and dangerously preoccupied as they find a seat in the congregation. Matters of their very spiritual health are at stake. Entreating their participation and summoning their focus just became exponentially more challenging!
- **The relative busyness of the congregant's professional/private life:** The more demanding one's private life becomes for business or personal reasons, the less time is given for the preparation of the heart before a service begins. Translation: Busyness is a dramatic distraction in twenty-first-century life all across the globe. Worship leaders need to have listened to the Spirit in the preparation phase and arranged the flow of the worship in meticulous detail in the planning phase.
- **The stress-filled nature of the commute to church:** Scripture says, "The adversary seeks whom He may devour" (1 Peter 5:8). Wherever there is a car or a family involved in getting ready for and traveling to church, there exists the possibility of strife. Someone spills, someone teases, and then someone loses his or her temper. The car won't start. Someone cuts the family off on a highway. Attitudes suddenly shift. Words are hastily spoken. Forgiveness is not sought in time, as the vehicle turns into the parking lot. Then, of course, the lot is full, and the list is endless, but the reality of entering onto holy ground, rattled by the devil's plot and ploy, is entirely problematic. The mental gymnastics of getting children to classes and a couple to find harmony again is time-consuming. If the enemy can keep us left-footed enough so that the worship goes by in a perfunctory rather than in a catalytic manner, we lose a precious opportunity to engage in Spirit-filled life.

The inability of a congregant to exhale—once having entered sacred space to focus intently on ministering to the Lord—is an all-too-often overlooked phenomenon. It is at once costly and prohibitive to one's spiritual growth. Accordingly, believers have to be alert. On guard! We need to be ready to participate and fully cognizant of the precious opportunity before us to minister to the Lord, but that is a mind-set. It must be taught in perhaps a yearly sermon on essentials of Christianity and the value of corporate worship.

Preparation is a hard-won skill. The worship leader has to carefully choose the songs in just the right order. Then decisions have to be made with regard to pacing the songs so as to allow the congregation to grow comfortable enough to forget the stress and minister to the Savior.

Meanwhile, the congregant must arise early enough to prepare the heart before waking the children. They must attend to the mechanics of the car the day before. They must consider the family's routine and be organized, not sporadic. They must pray in the car and listen to the kind of music that will be soothing. They must leave early in anticipation of traffic or chaos.

On both sides of the spectrum—the musician's platform awareness and the congregant's pew responsibility—the same willfulness is called to attention. Behold! Sunday is the Lord's day. Act accordingly.

- **The worship leader's ability to countermand the distractions of modern worship:** Worship trendiness dictates matters of song selection, stage presence, and fashion that are appropriate for the Sunday worship experience. If being cute is the agenda, many chief musicians buy into thinking if the sound is tight and the look is bright, they have done their job. However, attention to the latest trend can be counterproductive. Beyond accommodating the latest fad in leading worship, we cannot overlook the work of the Spirit. Being a prepared servant musically, while being careless spiritually, is a recipe for short-term success and longer-term congregational apathy.

- **The priceless musical ability to transition from one song to another without digital inaccuracies:** There is no substitute for mastering an instrument and playing in such a way that the congregation can relax and place their attention on the Lord. If the music is too loud, the transition from one song to another too abrupt or too long or the tempos are not in the pocket, a congregant will have to note the musical confusion and play mental gymnastics to find the pathway into the realm of the spirit all over again. That is just not acceptable.

Necessary Skills Incumbent upon the Serious Worship Leader

Worship is a high priority in heaven. Just read the book of Revelation. In heaven, matters of attitude and atmosphere take on cosmic proportion. No detail is omitted. Excellence is noticeable everywhere. Clearly there is power in the throne room that flows unabated.

Can that be said of the chancel in the church you serve? To become all that God wants of our leadership as church musicians, you and I must manage our growth and development carefully.

A schoolteacher does. After college, there are innumerable in-service programs to master, new and ever-changing curriculums to internalize, jargon-intensive procedures to update, and regular observations by the administration to pass.

A physician does. After medical school, there is an internship to matriculate. There are strict board exams to pass and endless journal articles to comprehend. One cannot be a physician today without considerable computer acumen as well. For the frenetic pace of technological change in the medical profession, worldwide, is daunting.

What happens to a worship leader? After being appointed, what criterion is expected in order to develop one's skills as a pastor, counselor, musician, artist, worship leader, and, most importantly, a man or woman of God?

There is a seasoning that must take place in a worship leader's life. This process requires maturity in the personal domain, competency in the musical domain, mastery in the leadership domain, and a well-developed work ethic in the domain of the Holy Ghost. Becoming an adult is not about reaching a particular age, but about learning that one of the secrets of adulthood is finally understanding that love is about giving, not taking. It is about realizing that love's ally, loyalty, is a two-way street and that love's essence, trust, is earned. Longevity on a pastoral staff is driven, in large part, by our attitude as pastoral staff.

Matters of Attitude

One's personal attitude, like motivation, is a critically important inward choice that has potent outward benefits. Choose now to develop a positive attitude. Let that attitudinal mind-set encompass the following cluster of winning behaviors:

1. Choose to reverence the Lord in word and deed.
2. Choose to be a team player at all times, no matter who receives the credit.
3. Choose to honor the Lord with the firstfruits of your time, talent, and resources.
4. Choose to become a disciplined, lifelong learner, beginning with the reading of the Word on a daily basis.
5. Choose to forgive before the offensive statement being said of or to you is even fully articulated.
6. Choose to monitor your entertainment choices.
7. Choose to be loyal and kind, even if your supervisor, pastor, or bishop does not respond in kind.
8. Choose to avoid favoritism among your peers and subordinates. Treat all you serve with equal portions of dignity and respect. Don't let your worship team's poor attitude affect your response to their immaturity or carnality. The way of the Lord is a process. Someone was patient with you.
9. Choose to guard your tongue, avoiding gossip at all costs. Gossip is cancerous. Be the chemotherapy in your ministry!
10. Choose to work hard. Laziness abounds in the profession of the ministry. Don't become a statistic! Paying attention to the slightest detail only makes you stronger for the increasingly evil days ahead.

Ultimately choose to serve the Lord in worship. It is about Him, not you. Do what He says. Choose the repertoire He anoints. Ask what would please Him each Sunday. Then try your best to balance the fad or trend of the day with the eternal. At best, a trend is a minor consideration. Your spiritual health, however, and your ability to engage in or invoke the presence of the Lord matters far more than your attire, light show, or cool stage presence.

Matters of Atmospherics

By atmospherics, I am referring both to the look of your space and the feel of your space. One of my mentors used to say, "Keep your office, rehearsal hall, and chancel neat at all times. The devil hangs around the trash!" While that remark was said with a measure of jest, I never forgot the pungency of his utterance. There is merit indeed in keeping a working environment clean and organized.

If my desk or prayer closet is messy, I do not focus as well as if it is pristine. If the rehearsal hall is sloppy with wrappers about and music disheveled, it is hard to focus on the things of the Lord. If the chancel is dirty, like a hospital, how can people who are sick receive wholesome "medical" treatment?

I believe a sanctuary is a hospital. The prayer room is the ER. The congregational seats are the surgery rooms, and the chancel itself is where the doctors gather to confer as to which procedure is optimal for the health of the body. Cleanliness is paramount in a hospital. In a toxic environment, people who are sick will become more infected by virtue of the atmospherics present.

Please pause for a moment to let this metaphor internalize in your spirit. Ask yourself, "How toxic is my environment?" Would you stop and consider your answer with introspection and honesty before the Lord? If the atmosphere is pleasing to the

> *Be like Jesus!*

Lord, people who attend will naturally find answers to their questions and peace for the storms of life that beguile them. Unfortunately, the converse is also true.

A Spirit-led musician will positively affect the atmosphere of the church. Everywhere Jesus trod, miracles ensued. Every time He spoke, peace invaded the atmosphere. Jesus constantly turned a wrong into a right! He touched the unlovely with grace. He offered untold mercy to the lost, the disenfranchised, and those in despair. He was light in darkness. He was hope amid fear. He was love to those left behind.

Let His gentle ways revolutionize your growing edges. All of us are broken to some extent. We all slip. We all fail. We all miss the mark. The only flawless, faultless man in history was our Lord Jesus. Strangely enough though, even though He never failed, the Bible says, "He is touched with the feelings of our infirmity" (Hebrews 4:15). He is empathic. He is all loving. He is the personification of forgiveness.

If we have done our due diligence to keep the spaces of worship immaculate and with equal measure, our hearts soft before Him, everything else as pastoral musicians will fall into place. Grace and peace. A time of journal writing or prayerful thought might be in order before continuing to read this chapter.

Matters of Practices

Now let's turn our attention to the practical dimensions of creating a flow or medley of worship songs designed to let the congregation find peace with God. I affirm that the congregational singing in the church should encompass two distinct times of expression.

In the opening songs, the attention should be exclusively placed on God Almighty. In Psalm 100, we are encouraged to "come into His presence with singing." Those critical opening songs should welcome Him by honoring His Name.

After the invocation and reading of scripture and other church orders of business, I support taking a second period of time to seek the Lord on behalf of the needs of the congregation through song. This second opportunity to commune with the Lord in worship requires the skillful touch of a surgeon.

Each song in the second phase of ministry must be handled with care. Conceptually, these songs should be designed to allow congregants a chance to talk with the Lord, soften their hearts in His presence, inquire of His wisdom, and fall at His feet. As such, we need songs that move gently from theme to theme. Through repetition and thematic unity, the congregant has a chance to become intimate with Jesus. I love what T. D.

Jakes, the prominent American pastor, says about intimacy. He defines the term as, "Into me see!"

The process of moving busy, preoccupied people into a moment of transparency—in divine presence—is easier said than done. However, it is achievable with prayerful attention and careful rehearsal. Once I have listed the songs for worship, I pause to read the songs aloud. I ask myself:

- Do the lyrics complement each other?
- Do they incrementally move the theme forward?
- Is the forward movement measurable? In other words, can I perceive the pathway from outer court to inner court in clear steps?
- Have I done everything in my capacity to turn my eyes toward heaven before the Sunday service? Can I, in fact, hear the "still, small voice" the people so desperately need in real time during the service?
- Am I sensitive enough to the voice of the Spirit that I can make an immediate change in my plan? Should I feel His check in my spirit?

Once I feel comfortable with the lyrical flow, I turn my attention to the methodology of the musical transition out of one song and into the next. I ask:

- Is each transitional element smooth?
- Are the meters compatible?
- Is there a need to modulate? If so, how economically can that musical process be done?
- Is there room to linger? If so, what kind of pad will be appropriate?
- At what point do we transition to the God moment?

The God moment is what I refer to as the celebration that God is in our midst and has heard our cry for help or received our thanksgiving. Sometimes in a God moment, there will be a manifestation of the Spirit. Other times there will be a call for salvation or a time of spontaneous prayer at the altar. Still other times, there will be a word of edification from the pastor. In any event, all will know that we have truly been in the presence of the King.

Some years ago, I was speaking in a church in central California on a Sunday evening. After being introduced, I led a season of worship from the piano before stepping into the pulpit to preach. During the worship, I mistakenly thought about trying to impress the people by moving from the song we were currently experiencing into the next song through a sudden leap to a higher key.

I mused, "Won't they be impressed by this musical act of daring?"

All of a sudden, I sensed the hand of God on my shoulder and a word of admonition just as clear as a bell. The Spirit said, "Tom, is it really that important to you to *show off*, or would it be all right with you if I just *showed up* instead?"

I was devastated. How could I have been so foolish and prideful? After teaching on matters related to worship for many years, how could I be so needy as to use worship for man's applause? Immediately I repented. We had a dynamic service, and I never attempted a musical feat like that again.

What is the moral of that story? At worship's core, there is a mix of man's talent and God's supreme ability to enter in on a song with healing in His wings. The former is only a tool. The latter is a priceless work of art. Don't confuse them. We serve. We open a door. We facilitate. We guide. We set a table. We welcome, but it is He who does the work.

> *Composer Matt Redman said it best, "Don't let the work of the Lord overcome the Lord of the work!"*

This is true in our private life and, most assuredly, in our public life as well. Our goal is found in Zephaniah 3:17. "The Lord your God is in your midst, the Mighty one will save; He will rejoice over you with gladness, He will quiet you with His love, He will rejoice over you with singing."

Seeds from the Core

1. Worship leading involves knowing how to choose songs, teach them effectively, and place them in a meaningful sequence (a flow).

Then the congregation can find an intimacy with Christ as they participate in corporate worship encounters.

2. Choosing songs for worship is a multifaceted decision that is best made in a prayerful state before the Lord.

3. Creating a flow of worship presupposes lyrical considerations, musical sensitivity, and a keen ear to the Spirit.

4. Keeping all generations on the same page is a critical component of the worship leader's intercession. Unity brings the anointing, and the anointing sets the captives free.

Most people do not see things as they ARE
because they see things as THEY are!

—Richard Rohr

CHAPTER 7

THE ONE THING

A chapter in a book on leading worship that centers on the behind-the-scenes relationship between the pastor and worship leader is almost a cliché. Much has been written on this subject. Yet, from my perspective, there is more to be said. To begin, here's what we know:

- **All human beings develop a point of view.** However, a point of view is really just a view from a point. To successfully build a team of pastors unified by missional objectives, one has to enlarge his or her worldview to consider the divergent points of view each colleague has. No one has the full picture! Collaboration is optimal. We need each other.
- **In marriage, opposites frequently attract.** After the vows and the reception, couples then have to learn to cope. No wonder between 40 to 50 percent of marriages fail. Marriage requires coping, adapting, understanding, forgiving, refusing to become bitter or hold a grudge, choosing to believe the best, and actively memorizing the other sacred words of 1 Corinthians 13. These are critical elements of longevity not only in a marriage but in the pastoral staff environment as well.
- **The statistics on worship leader tenure are bleak.** Worship leader tenure is on average between eighteen to twenty-four

months. This is pathetic and dangerous to the health of a body of believers. Dare we ask why?

- **Pastors are many times bold leaders who had difficult parents.** If a pastor grew up in a dysfunctional home, chances are, he or she treats his or her staff in a similar manner. Most worship leaders do not know about this neurotic syndrome until faced with an irregular leader who functions on Sunday with authority and biblical prowess while treating the staff during the week with frozen feelings and ill will and at times is suspicious, aloof, and foreboding.

Herein is one of the chief ironies of pastoral life in the twenty-first-century church. The one thing a worship leader needs is a pastor who understands him or her. Yet, if the pastor is wounded or broken by an all-too-often troubled childhood, he or she has little bandwidth left to empathize with the staff.

Leaders who have experienced difficult childhoods often choose a helping profession in order to work through their repressions. The ministry is no exception. By helping people less fortunate than themselves, they seem to believe they will earn a pardon from God. It is entirely possible for these kinds of leaders to be sympathetic to the stranger yet unsympathetic toward their associates. Innocent church musicians walk into this emotional buzz saw and never see the wounds coming. After serving in church after church to no avail, disillusionment mounts. Ultimately worship leaders exit the ministry, feeling like a failure.

> *Could this be the ultimate ploy of the adversary, who was expelled from heaven for wanting to steal the Lord's glory? Could he be jealous of any worship leader who breaks through this bondage and builds a fruitful musical ministry?*

Soberly, I begin this chapter calling you to consider your call to ministry with careful, deliberate, and reflective prayer. Working with leaders who carry baggage is not easy. In Christian service, there are traps to avoid and pitfalls to elude. By traps, I am essentially referring to the temptations of pride and self-reliance. Pride dictates a certain dependence on one's gifting and thereby ignoring the need for earnest prayer and communion. However, "prayerlessness leads to carelessness."[13] One matter related to being careless has to do with a musician's propensity to think he or she alone is responsible for his or her talent.

Humility, by contrast, seems to be the way our Lord managed life. "Let us decrease so He may increase" (John 3:30) is a preferred way to gain the admiration of man and the anointing of our Master. Dependence on the Holy Spirit and regular communion with Jesus, our Lord and

> *An oversized ego creates havoc in the ministry of music.*

Savior, are the foundational underpinnings on which one builds a ministry. Our so-called righteousness, our inherent gifts, and our capacities fall short of ministry effectiveness without the Master's touch.

By pitfalls, I am referring to the unforeseen duplicity that exists in unhealthy pastoral staff environments where the corporate culture of the church is laden with conflict. Conflicts that are not brought to the light of day and properly resolved only serve to boomerang. Dark conversations spread like wildfire. The net result is gossip, enmity, and ultimately disloyalty. Once a pastoral

> *When conflicts within pastoral staff environment are left unattended, the home church culture grows toxic.*

person begins to traffic in those modalities, the work of the ministry takes on an infection.

Into this tenuous scene emerges a worship leader whose singular need is for the pastor to provide a covering of understanding that contains elements of caring, support, advocacy, and guidance to shape them into authentic, lifelong church musicians. Instead these innocent young musicians frequently find themselves subordinated to a fast-paced, top-down, autocratic church culture of "do as I say, not as I do."

I believe this scenario does not have to be your future because knowledge is power. Having been forewarned, let's assume you know

---

[13] Norman Shawchuck and Roger Heuser, *Loading the Congregation* (Nashville: Abingdon Press, 1993), 39.

how to interview while being interviewed. Through dialogue, you need to be able to detect if the potential pastor is not only healthy but in the ministry for altruistic reasons. Remember the words of Edwin Cole, "Peace is the umpire of God's will." An interview without the commensurate complement of peace should cause you to run! By the same token, if you do feel the pastor is healthy and the presence of peace invades your dialogue, see those factors as a green light to move forward.

The 60/40 Principle

That being said, following are aspects of leading worship written specifically for pastors to review in order to assist the godly nurturing process of a worship leader. If a pastor will invest in a worship leader's spiritual formation and leadership development, the staff will solidify, the church will grow, and all will experience grace.

I have been deeply moved this year by the in-service component of being a public schoolteacher. Among the cutting-edge trends in pedagogy today is a new emphasis to make the classroom commodious to the learning process, especially for students with whom English is a second language.

Teachers in Los Angeles are now being encouraged to adopt a 60/40 model for the acquisition of classroom knowledge. In short, this means that teachers are to plan academic activities for 60 percent of the week while giving up to 40 percent of their time and attention to matters related to the affective domain.

The *affective domain* is a term that identifies the student's need to feel safe and welcomed, validated, and assured that his or her opinions and queries are heard. Adjusting the instruction to accommodate the affective domain presupposes that the learner be more involved in classroom procedures. In other words, students from problematic community environments do not always learn best by lecture or reading from the textbook exclusively. Discussions and other interactive protocols are critically important for at-risk students.

For example, discovery through participation in a carefully prearranged game or by sitting in a circle sharing answers to precisely developed questions is becoming increasingly powerful as a means of clarifying concepts and internalizing burgeoning belief systems.

Another word for this educational trend is *restorative justice.* In a multicultural classroom, all students matter. All deserve respect, recognition, and righteous consideration regardless of economic status or heritage. The classroom is to be a special place where learners are actively restored out of poverty

> Someone aptly said, "When the teacher stops talking, the students start learning."

and into the possibility of a transformational learning setting that at once lifts the spirit, incites curiosity, and replaces despair with hope. This new trend is called restorative justice. The five tenets of a restorative classroom include:

- Respect—being mindful of everyone around you; valuing his or her uniqueness
- Relationship building—promoting peaceful friendships; practicing active listening
- Responsible actions—transforming the classroom environment by our contributions and peacekeeping
- Repair—caring for the needs of others through understanding and kindness without judgment
- Reintegration—committing to the challenge of helping others find redemption and a more preferable future

One of the authors of the restorative justice movement, Marianne Williamson, concludes, "In every community there is work to be done … wounds to heal."

Taking off my educational hat and speaking as a pastoral mentor, let me say that a worship team rehearsal could very effectively be managed in a similar way. There should be time in a weekly rehearsal to learn vocal technique to be sure. Time has to be allotted to manage the presenting tasks of music ministry: master new songs, practice the flow of worship for the next gathering, and intercession for the ongoing mission of the church. These matters could effectively be termed the 60 percent, if you will.

Moreover, worship leaders should also be mindful of the atmosphere of the rehearsal space. This is the category of the affective domain. Caring for the individual needs of the membership is a strategic factor in the development of healthy worship team members. Having time allotted to practice the presence of the Lord in rehearsal, making time to testify, offering prayer requests, and being enriched by a devotional are ways to minister healing to the soul and recovery to the oppressed.

In short, the rehearsal should be musically fulfilling and spiritually enlivening. Singers and players should leave feeling better than when they arrived. Members should grow to understand they matter, belong, and are necessary for the team to succeed. This then is the 40 percent component of administering a restorative rehearsal environment.

In the end, the role of worship leader is a divine trust among a church musician, the congregation, and the Lord. Beyond the task of leading worship on Sunday, a congregation deserves a candidate who, throughout the week, is a capable and trusted leader. The aegis of this office is multifaceted, including matters of spiritual formation, musical mastery, and emotional intelligence.

Pastors should be aware of the challenges inherent in making a rehearsal inspiring. The congregation should also be aware of the vast skill set necessary to achieve mastery of the eight essential competencies, so they can partner with the pastor in praying for the worship leader.

Eight Essential Worship Leader Competencies

Following are eight distinct areas of competency all worship leaders should master. Each has four stages. Together, they form the composite job description. All pastors should be aware of these domains of effectiveness designed to enrich a congregation and provide a standard for worship leader achievement and advancement.

An Ability to Accept Responsibility

- To honor the Lord in word and deed
- To be loyal to the pastor
- To be prepared for Sunday and in rehearsal
- To be like Jesus in matters of interpersonal relationship

When a worship leader accepts this office, he or she is saying, in effect, he or she will do everything possible to honor the Lord in each of the aforementioned categories. To honor is to put first. The idea is that a worship leader who prioritizes the things of God in terms of how he or she thinks, behaves, and interacts away from the spotlight sets in motion God's blessing and anointing. Credibility in ministry is directly related to the proper management of one's private life.

What's more, in any professional relationship loyalty is a premium. Loyalty is an essential, but loyalty is a two-way street. To function optimally, both the pastor and the worship leader must demonstrate faithfulness and trustworthiness. All of hell wants to thwart the work of ministry worldwide. There cannot be even the slightest kink in pastoral relationships, or the adversary will take advantage.

The enemy and his minions move in the arena of rumor and innuendo. These inky impressions include falsehoods, misrepresentations, and brutal forms of character assassination. Beyond that, the sycophants of hell seize on unresolved misunderstandings and hurt feelings. They brood in the minds of the offended. However, the good news is the scriptures are potent. The Word of God, once invoked, always sweeps the floor, reframes the brain, and provides a way of escape (1 Corinthians 10:13).

When slighted in a staff meeting or offended by a petty criticism in the foyer of the building, they quickly arise and quote a scripture or sing a song. The adversary will readily flee when a worship leader is proactive.

Please say these verses out loud and loudly:

- "Greater is He that is in [me] than he that is in the world" (1 John 4:4).
- "I can do all things through Christ who strengthens me" [including forgiving my colleagues] (Philippians 4:13).
- "It is not by might, nor by power, but by my Spirit, says the Lord of Hosts" (Zechariah 4:6).

There is great relief available to a pastoral musician who understands spiritual warfare and makes a daily priority to keep the heart soft and the memory short. Forgiving misunderstandings is essential to obtaining peace in the work of the ministry.

Another value I affirm with regard to accepting responsibility for the health of the body is a well-developed work ethic. There can be no excuse for unpreparedness in a worship leader's public presentation. The flock deserves respect as evidenced by not wasting their time on Sunday.

Don't bore them with vain repetitions. Don't put them to sleep with circuitous introductions of new songs. Don't appear in sloppy garb or, more importantly, in a state of spiritual confusion, about your purpose of the worship you're about to lead.

Attention to detail and a positive attitude are indispensable traits in terms of being prepared. Being prepared is not only a musical consideration but a temperament concern as well. A musician must function with style and grace at an instrument and, simultaneously, be in control of his or her spirit.

Lastly, to serve a church as worship leader, the office holder must commit to managing interpersonal relationships with circumspect transparency and ethical purity.

An Aptitude to Exceed Expectations

- To be fluent in musical theory and practice
- To be mature in matters of Kingdom conduct
- To be kind to all
- To be on task, in the game, and not looking over one's shoulder

Musical proficiency is a given in today's high-tech environment. People hear excellent music in the simplest of commercials or the scariest of movies. How can we expect seekers to frequent our church if the performance practice of the worship team is subpar?

Beyond musical excellence, an excellent spirit is also a factor in this discussion. Matters of Kingdom conduct include a study of the way in which our Lord Jesus managed His ministry. He was attentive to the unlovely, the alien, and the disenfranchised. He turned the other cheek when He could have easily lashed out. He offered a cup of cold water

> *Jesus's shining example is worthy of a lifetime of study, introspection, and modeling.*

to the thirsty no matter who they were. He was the penultimate example of the practice of patience.

While introspecting about the model of Jesus's life, let integrity infuse both your present and your future. It is wholly unprofessional to use the church in which you are now serving to catapult you into a bigger church. Stay on task! Be faithful. Do not worry about tomorrow. Rather, remember, "Promotion comes from the Lord" (Psalm 75:6).

A Choice to Embrace Protocols

- To be succinct in public and confidential in private
- To be positive in attitude and professional in garb
- To avoid the appearance of evil in the community
- To carefully balance the use of repertoire and instrumentation

Pastors hire us to sing, not preach. Please respect that distinction. Function in the realm of your specific portfolio. Bring excellence to that role. Bloom where planted. Blooming has implications that are professional and applications that are personal. Private life choices with regard to entertainment can be thorny, so choose the high road. Be careful, ever mindful not to cause a brother or sister to falter by your appetites.

Finally I believe a worship leader is responsible to program worship materials that minister to each generation and ethnicity in the church. As you are inclusive, your ministry will gain a stride that can only be defined as "God's favor," for God is attentive to the lowest common denominator in the room. You should be too.

A Capacity to Accommodate Disciplines

- To be curious about life and, more importantly, life in the Kingdom
- To contend in the Spirit: souls, vision casting, and anointing
- To be a lifelong learner: musically, academically, and spiritually
- To be a team player: sharing everything you know with everyone you have

These four criteria presuppose a dogged determination to be the very best one can be for Jesus, who gave up everything for us. Making room in our lives for personal disciplines, out of devotion, is one of the most sacred decisions a worship leader can make. Life in ministry is not so much about what you and I can't do, but what we choose to lay down so Jesus can occupy a fuller focus.

Interestingly, when Jesus finally becomes our entirety, our ministry morphs. Greater insights occur, greater self-control is noticed, and a greater passion for the lost is established. Wendell Berry would concur, writing, "By restraint we are made whole."

Therefore, I encourage you to reflect on these spiritual ideas with a contrite heart for the Bible is clear, "Take up your cross and follow me" (Matthew 16:24). This is the mark of discipleship. Those who forsake earthly ease for the Master will doubtless receive blessings untold. Jesus

> *Without a doubt, personal sacrifices spawn ministry enhancement.*

has a way of caring for the devoted that defies explanation. His blessing is found in a myriad of little things in our private lives that run more smoothly, last longer, stay healthier, and, when needed, are suddenly on sale. There is nothing quite like following in the way of the Lord.

Finally, with regard to the concept of pastoral team interactions, let me be transparent. Early in my ministry, I served with a very competitive colleague. He was gifted and charismatic. His program grew by leaps and bounds. Yet he had a problem with sharing. He struggled to share his personnel, give another leader credit in a meeting, and was always

> *Father James Keller said, "A candle that lights another loses nothing."*

trying to compete with my results after a festive holiday event. Don't become *that* guy!

A Heart to Receive Correction

- To admit mistakes and to avoid cover-ups
- To cover the pastor, your colleagues, and your family

- To discipline carefully, avoid favoritism, and employ unconditional positive regard
- To be submitted on matters of service order, church goals, and senior or lead pastor objectives

A mature leader always takes responsibility for mistakes and misunderstandings. To admit one's error and ask for forgiveness is a deeply restorative activity for the worship team to practice, employ, and habituate. The Word reminds us, "Forgive and you will be forgiven" (Matthew 6:14).

Second, the principle of unconditional positive regard deserves some context in our discussion. The educational psychologist, Carl Rogers, first coined this term to refer to the negative effect that a leader creates when he or she yells at a member of a group in front of the entire assemblage present in the room. Immediately the rest of the group shuts down for fear that if they do something wrong, they will be the next victim of the leader's wrath.

The whole matter of discipline in a worship team rehearsal is precarious. If a member of the team is out of order, being rude or disrespectful, it is much better to simply stop the activity, quietly ask for the offender to see you privately after the meeting, and regroup. Losing one's temper is never a good idea. This is especially true in the work of the ministry.

Along those same lines, the spiritual impact of submission can be a complex concept in today's culture. Submission, like loyalty, is a dual-lane highway. Being submitted to the pastor as worship leader is

> *Wrapped up in this milieu is a composite of attitudes: evenhandedness, deference, and pure love one for another.*

step one in receiving submission from your team. Moreover, submission is never given. It is earned. Submission presupposes trust. Trust presupposes fidelity.

A Belief in the Value of a Reward

- To be creative and fun
- To be fair

- To be consistent
- To model the principle of generosity

I am a big believer in taking the temperature of the rehearsal environment to heart. Of course, the comfort of the team with regard to air-conditioning in the summer or heat in the winter is a consideration. However, I'm referring more intently on the metaphoric atmosphere created by the people.

- To teach, the people in the room have to be in the right frame of mind.
- To share a devotional, the group in attendance must be prepared to receive the Word (always singing first).
- To cast vision, the mood of the room has to be faith-filled, engaged, and optimistic.

These traits of leadership sensitivity and careful preparation presuppose a value to be kind and thoughtful. At worship's core, the Spirit of Jesus must dominate the worship leader's soul since spirits reproduce after their own kind. Gentleness among the singers and players doesn't just manifest week by week without a leader who is setting that tone with consistency.

In my public school, all of the teachers begin each class by greeting every student at the door with a handshake and a personal greeting. I love this tradition! I can at once assess the mood of the student and set the pace for my day's procedures by simply looking into his or her eyes and saying something positive as each shuffles past.

> *Gentleness starts at the door.*

Beyond a pleasant greeting, I affirm the concept of 60/40 as discussed earlier in this chapter. Musical leaders who view the rehearsal solely as a task-oriented opportunity miss the mark. The ministry is about people. Performance practice is obviously essential but making music in a harsh environment seems counterintuitive. The ideal

> *I have always affirmed the words of Christian psychologist, Richard Dobbins, who said, "A healthy family is a noisy family!"*

rehearsal in a church environment is part task, part relationship building, part spiritual formation, and part fun! A worship team is a family of sorts.

Put simply, understanding the value of giving volunteers rewards as a criterion of the 40 percent domain is what Jesus would do with the disciples. He cared for their souls, in part, by caring for their appetites. Jesus was sensitive to every aspect of their lives, as He is today for ours. The gospel songwriter of old once penned, "It matters to Him about you!" For a partial list of the reward system I cultivated, please go to appendix2.

Ask the Lord for enhanced creativity! At all cost, avoid the mundane and the predictable, and you can be sure He is a "rewarder of those who seek Him diligently" (Hebrews 11:6).

A Proper Coda

- To realize that vocational ministry is seasonal, not eternal
- To be character-driven at the end of a season or assignment
- To be munificent in giving thanks for the opportunity and the people you served
- To make the transition smooth regardless of the circumstances

Saying good-bye has never been easy for me. I am sentimental. I value place, and I love people! When God has nudged my wife and me that a door is closing and a new window is opening, I approach those transitions with mixed emotion. I have learned by experience to walk through transitional moments cautiously.

For example, when leaving I carefully consider how I want to phrase the many good-byes. I will write thank-you notes by hand. I will walk through the sanctuary slowly for weeks prior to departing to personally thank the congregational members for their trust, cooperation, and kindness. To me, there is no more transparent illustration of a pastor's heart than in how he or she processes a final good-bye.

Hint: Make the whole transition about the people (their great sacrifices, their incredible buy-in, and their opportunity to continue to do great things for God and the Kingdom) and resist the temptation to brag or boast. No need for narcissism here.

Your promotion is not the burning issue with the congregation at hand. They are grieving. Your final act of their sacred trust is to assuage their loss with a professional, self-deprecating personal style. Be calm and equitable, reassuring and comforting. Remind them that better days are ahead. Above all, take the high road, especially with those who perhaps did not always agree with you.

A New Beginning

- To honor past achievements and prior leadership
- To be patient in making changes
- To respect the "clean slate" moment
- To commit to work hard, love people, and pursue excellence

Clean slate moments are all too rare. Value them by embracing the entire panoply of change, the good and the goofy, and the awkward and the challenging. If the clean slate moment is properly conceived, mindfully covered in prayer, and oh so carefully managed, the honeymoon in a new setting can be one of the most restful and fulfilling seasons of one's ministry vocation.

> *To start over is precious.*

In these moments, a church musician can recommit to a set of meaningful core values and practice them anew with greater passion. One can also regroup emotionally in a transition observing a deeper consecration to God, family, and one's call. It will be weeks before the calendar begins to pull and push again.

Make a priority of caring for your spouse. Fall in love again. Remember why you married that amazing individual. Care for your health. Exercise

> *During the respite when all is unfamiliar, focus on the familiar!*

more regularly. Read more, listen more, and practice more. Improve a growing edge as though you were on a summer hiatus from university and take advantage of this new but fleeting freedom. I love the clean slate moment!

However, there is one caveat. Be careful not to bring tired, old habits along with you in your new setting. Introspect. What from your last assignment did not go as planned? How can you improve in that area of your skill set? What are the pitfalls when starting over?

Look deeper until you are familiar with a new congregation and practice interpersonal self-discipline. Beware of the early individuals who flatter you in the church. They may be vying for control later on. Refuse to entertain anyone who wants to complain about the pastor. That is playing with fire! Be kind to all, but be cautious. Hold off on choosing personal friends until the dust settles.

In closing, the Eight Worship Leader Competencies are a structure for pastor and worship leader to process together. They are a framework for creating and enriching a lifelong ministry. Each construct is potent in the realm of the spirit. Adapted over time, a teachable worship leader who has been tested, seasoned, and spiritually formed will become a fruitful servant leader in the Kingdom of God.

Taking a youthful worship leader through the paces toward maturity is a priceless gift a compassionate pastor bestows on his or her young colleague. When you find such a leader, put roots down and stay for a while. The shaping of a gifted teaching pastor is invaluable. I submit these factors for your ministry preparation with the hope that you will become all that God intended. May His grace shine on you in ever increasing ways!

Ten Ways to Enhance Morale[14]

Over the course of my ministry, I have worked with thousands of volunteers. All were motivated. All wanted to make a difference. All started from a perspective of enthusiasm, at least at first. However, ministry is dusty. Dirt and debris clog our pores, and after a while, we need to shower in Jesus's love and forgiveness.

Following are ten ways to do just that! Please note that this portion of the chapter is written to a bifurcated audience: the worship leader and the team member.

As we mature in our capacity to lead worship, there will come a day in which we discover just how important interpersonal factors are when a ministry group gathers to improve. This is the essence of servant leadership.

---

[14] From an article I wrote for an Assemblies of God magazine in the early 2000s.

1. *Be like Jesus:* This is a mantra for me. Jesus was always patient amid a storm. He was always kind amid criticism. He was always gentle amid the disenfranchised. He guarded His temper. He left a room brighter than when He entered. If we could grasp a vision of Jesus's way of being, we would make the ministry of music sparkle!

2. *Be on time:* Nothing deflates morale like team member tardiness. It interrupts flow. It distracts attention. It breaks down esprit de corps. Frankly, it is a harmful habit. Once you open the door to being late, sooner or later you will rationalize that behavior for every appointment of your life.

    The discipline required to order one's life around promptness is an asset. Being prompt is a discipline. Being on time is also a gift you give your leader. If you are on time, your worship leader can focus on the task and not on your anticipated late entrance.

    What's more, if the worship leader is tardy or sloppy beginning the rehearsal, a subtle message is sent to the membership that arriving casually is an acceptable behavior. Someone wisely said, "The greatest choral ability is dependability!"

3. *Be consistent:* One of the greatest threats to momentum is moodiness. If a team cannot be assured of one's even temper, the teammates may choose to either quit or ostracize the irregular volunteer. It is not fair to the group to walk on eggshells around an irregular volunteer. Dependent personalities drain the creativity and enthusiasm right out of a team.

    If you tend to react to life's challenges by pushing the anger button or transferring your irritation onto the innocent, the team will atrophy. This is true of the worship leader and the team members equally. A healthy worship team community casts their care on the Lord and not on each other!

4. *Be prepared:* The amount of time wasted in rehearsal by a vocalist or instrumentalists who did not properly prepare can never be

regained. Unnecessary review is boring. Even if you are not the most proficient person in the ensemble, you can greatly encourage your leader by showing up on task. As homework is a part of going to school, so preparation is a part of being on a worship team. There is a vast difference in a worship team who discerns the difference between practice and rehearsal. Practice is what happens in the woodshed, so to speak, apart from the public rehearsal. This is where individual members review songs, mastering melody or harmony, reviewing the phrasing structures, and committing the tune to memory. Rehearsal is about refining the choral tone, purifying the target sounds, synchronizing final consonants, and paying particular attention to the blend.

Preparation, therefore, is not only about learning music in a timely fashion but about adopting a positive attitude toward volunteerism as well. Each member can add value simply by purposing to be a help and not a hindrance while commuting to the rehearsal. Choose to be attentive. Choose to be cooperative. Choose to be a blessing!

These matters are all dealt with in the prayer closet. I have often mused at the difference between a member who comes to rehearsal on mission striving both to minister to the Lord and the team versus the ones who come to drain the life out of the team through the darker arts of gossip, fault finding, irritability, and antagonism.

5. *Be eager to share:* Young children, new Christians, and the insecure among us all face this challenge in life. It is easy to hoard; it is difficult to share. In a church department, some struggle to share a folder or a pencil. Others struggle to share the spotlight. Still more struggle to share their trials or temptations in a prayer time. When we share our need, we invoke the Kingdom. In that vulnerable moment, Jesus appears among us. If you have a need, share what you would like to receive and watch two things occur. First, you will bless your teammates. Second, God will smile and return the favor (Luke 6:38).

The same may be said of young pastoral teams. Often in a pack of newly minted leaders, one will rise above the flock to win the attention of the church by virtue of personality, charm, or work ethic. Others, like Joseph's brothers, may entertain jealousy and hinder the ministry by refusing to share equipment, advice, or personnel with the leader of the pack. Left unmanaged, the morale of the staff will plummet into toxicity. Beware. Guard your heart. Do the right thing, avoid the subterfuge, and let the Lord promote your efforts in due season.

6. *Be proactive:* A volunteer who enters a rehearsal hall with an eye toward finding a need and filling it for the benefit of the music ministry as a whole is a rare but useful individual.

In my Los Angeles choir, two ladies were ordinary musicians but extraordinary servants. One came early to rehearsal just to brew fresh coffee. The other wore a set of homemade bracelets under her robe during long concert runs. On this unique set of bracelets, she placed a row of cough lozenges, a row of aspirin, and a row of breath mints. These lovely ladies found a need on our team and filled it! Where's your niche?

7. *Be humble:* Humility is a practiced art. In part, humility is an intangible quality of character that motivates us to work hard, even if we never receive the credit. Humility will always gravitate toward service. To truly embrace humility as a behavioral choice is as elusive as finding contentment in whatever circumstance of life we happen to attain. A humble church musician will turn the other cheek, guard another's back, and ardently guide against stealing "the glory" in a moment of worship height. Humility breeds modesty. Modesty in words, actions, and attire always produces godly results.

I hunger to interact with humble persons when I travel as a pulpit guest. Here's the irony! Humble people attract both admiration from their peers and consideration from the Lord. "Humble yourself, under God's mighty, hand that He may lift you up" (1 Peter 5:6).

8. *Be musically intelligent:* Singers need to master choral tone in church. The smaller the ensemble, the more critical blend becomes. Tone quality is enhanced by a careful use of vibrato, a blending of registers, and a uniform approach to the production of vowel sounds. If properly rehearsed, these matters enhance the value of resonance.

   Players need to continue to study. A coach is necessary throughout one's career in music. We too easily develop bad habits, lose technique, and thereby become lazy. The antidote is simple: maintain a friendship with players in your town who are better than you are. Jam from time to time. Join a group that plays music in different styles. Just as the Lord wants to see you grow spiritually, He wants to observe the growth of your God-given talent too.

9. *Be spiritually sensitive:* Spirituality is defined by author Norman Shawchuck as "the means by which we develop an awareness of the presence of God in us and the process by which we keep that awareness fresh and vital." A praying member of the worship community, for example, is invaluable to the lead musician. Someone who knows how to touch God in a crisis moment can push back the adversary and foster breakthrough behind the scenes by invoking the Kingdom to guard and guide the worship leader, the worship team, and the whole church community.

   Prayer is more powerful than the onslaught of hell. Look at this promise, "People of Zion, who live in Jerusalem, you will weep no more. How gracious He will be when you cry for help! As soon as He hears, He will answer you" (Isaiah 30:19).

   Besides intercession, the worship team also benefits from the attitude of the team to comply when the worship leader invites the team to practice the presence of the Lord before they vocalize, offers a devotional study in the Word of God, or requests their attention in order to vision cast for the future.

These actions may appear to be simple matters of respect and paying attention, but I believe something deeper is at play in those moments. From my point of view, they suggest a reverence for the things of God. A cooperative attitude suggests a healthy view of submission. Where there is submission on a worship team, a divine covering develops over the whole process of preparing music for the Sunday worship encounters.

This is what it means to develop an awareness of the presence of God in rehearsal. Being sensitive to His entrance is everything! Sometimes His entrance is subtle, other times sudden. In other words, keeping our awareness fresh and vital in rehearsal is His invitation to join us as we rehearse. Truly, "They that wait on the Lord shall renew their strength" (Isaiah 40:31).

10. *Be lighthearted. Laugh!* Now no one likes a curmudgeon, but all respond to someone who has a sense of humor. Humor is caffeine to a rehearsal. It breaks tension and suddenly infuses the environment with laughter and goodness. Of course, timing is critical. Given that restraint, someone who is funny and knows the Ecclesial reference, "There is a time and place for everything … " (paraphrase, Ecclesiastes 3:1), adds a boost of energy to a rehearsal moment, lifting the morale and making the hard work at hand seem effortless.

These ten points have been offered to give insight to pastors who desire to encourage the ministry of the worship team. They are also offered to worship team members who, by reading this list, can engage in a deeper level of support for the worship leader's immense task.

We must remember that the preparing of worship is sacred and never forget who the songs are for or how complex the preparation. If the worship experience is free from distraction and goes well on Sunday, the people can find relief, comfort, forgiveness, and peace. Then the church takes on a transcendence unlike any other gathering known to man. Could anything be more exquisite?

Revisiting the One Thing

Sadly, when congregational singing does go well, it is perceived that the event was relatively simple to accomplish. However, that is a misnomer because behind the scenes a war rages for the souls of men and women every time a church gathers to worship God. The scriptures declare, "Our struggle is not against flesh and blood, but against the rulers, against the authorities, against the powers of this dark world and against the spiritual forces of evil in high places" (Ephesians 6:12). The Sunday worship encounter is a critical component in the strategy of heaven to win the lost, redeem their past, and usher seekers into new life in Christ.

That is why we are buffeted by the adversary and battered about by human personality conflict. The former is won in prayer. The latter is won through conflict resolution, anger management, emotional intelligence, and lifelong learning. Above all, I believe a close, impenetrable bond must be created between Jesus, the pastor, and the worship leader. Remember, "The three-strand cord is not easily broken" (Ecclesiastes 4:12).

Part of the bonding process between the principal leaders involves a willingness to have each other's back in controversy and share leadership concepts freely in staff meetings. If a pastor can lead this charge and extend mercy to the staff through a careful understanding of both the person of the worship leader and the practice of the art of leading worship,

> *This is worth fighting for! Congregational stability is at risk.*

harmony can prevail, and longevity becomes a distinct possibility. In an era of hasty worship leader transition, the promise of a pastor and worship leader actually working through their issues rather than walking away from them seems ideal.

How can they focus on God if the leaders who guide them are destabilized every twenty-four months? A congregation longs for staff cooperation. Believers come to a church to commune with God, to grow, to ponder life's difficult choices, and to find peace. If trust can be built between the staff and the congregation and the leaders are in one accord, the works of hell may be kept at bay and the distractions of staff conflict minimalized. Only then can a celebrant be freed to worship.

The many concepts of this chapter were derived from my university lectures and birthed in demanding ministry trials throughout the span of my career. They were hard-won lessons I processed in the furnace. The refiner's fire is a priceless though painful process to which all serious church musicians must submit in order to grow. However, after the fire comes a new understanding and a rich contentment. "Old things pass away; behold all things become new" (2 Corinthians 5:17).

> *Robert Schuller famously noted, "Tough times don't last but tough people do!"*

I submit these constructs to you as a gift. They are the result of a loving dialogue between God and His ofttimes idiosyncratic pupil. In the end, I assure you, the way of the Lord works. Don't be afraid of the tough times.

Seeds from the Core

1. Pastors who have experienced a troubled home life as children often relate to the church associates with frozen feelings. This matter is completely redeemable through grace.

2. In order to provide the worship leader, the one thing necessary to be fruitful on staff, pastoral understanding and support, it may be helpful for all to review the list of eight worship leader competencies together.

3. Worship team morale is vital to keep the team unified, prayerful, and pleasant.

4. The battle behind the scenes rages, but "Greater is He that is within us than he that is in the world" (1 John 4:4).

I am sure that God who began the good work in you will keep on working in you until the day that Jesus Christ comes again.

—Philippians 1:6

CHAPTER 8

APPROACHING THE DEVOTIONAL MOMENT

The thought of asking a worship team to listen to us teach from the Bible is daunting. I clearly remember my first pastor gathering our young, fledgling group of associates in his office each day for morning devotions. I was recently hired full time to direct the music at the church. Altogether there were four of us in those days.

The senior minister convened an hour-long meeting each morning that was catalytic in my young ministerial life. Part of each meeting included fellowship, calendar planning, and prayer for the church. In general, this was a team-building convocation. Those items would have been enough to serve as a catalyst in doctrine, Christian formation, and servant leadership, but there was more. Much more!

In addition, this wise leader set in motion another component, which at first I dreaded. I'm referring to the opening segment of our daily staff meeting—the shared devotional. Each week for years, our pastor invited the three of us to lead one morning meditation each week. We were to announce a text, cultivate a title, and share the text's meaning for our colleagues' growth and development. I was petrified! All of my colleagues had religious training. Two had been to seminary, and their presentations were rich and interesting. Then there was mine. I was a complete neophyte.

My most vivid remembrance of those growth years is the fact that as soon as I mentioned the text, the guys would begin to quote the scripture itself or process a brief anecdote about the text. Although funny now, in those days I was sorely intimidated by Thursday morning and my meager attempt to lead the devotional.

I tell this story for two reasons. First, I want all of my readers to know that the Lord does not "despise the day of a small beginning" (Zechariah 4:10). Second, I hope that pastors and worship leaders in churches across the globe will take a page from my former colleague's book and think seriously about holding a daily staff meeting for the purpose of discipling a burgeoning staff.

You see, my public speaking improved with practice and the loving support of the people in the room. Perhaps more importantly, I matured by quantum leaps in the development of a theology of Christian service because of the patience of my first pastor. He insightfully conducted a master class in how to pastor a congregation. I was attending seminary and did not even realize it at the time. Because of his understanding of the ministry, coupled with his care for us, his young disciples learned to respect the voice of the Shepherd, develop invaluable leadership skills, and by God's grace, grow a choir of two hundred voices that touched an entire city. I served with Dr. Earl Baldwin for twenty years.

As such, I have a deep respect for the process of becoming a servant leader in a church. Raising a young worship leader in the things of God is a sensitive task that presupposes seasoning, nurturance, and careful, deliberate counsel.

The Moment of Personal Reflection

In this chapter, our focus is on the rehearsal's *Moment of Personal Reflection* in the scriptures. Not every rehearsal needs a formal devotion for obvious reasons.

For example there are brief sound checks prior to a service in which a prayer of welcoming the presence of the Lord suffices. There are dress rehearsals prior to a holiday concert in which a gentle smile and warm greeting sets the tone for the technical work ahead. There are team gatherings for social events or congratulatory occasions in which team building activities prevail.

That being said, I encourage all to bake into the rehearsal schedule regular times for introspection, Holy Spirit fullness, and spiritual formation amid the rigors of note reading, vocalization, and the development of choral tone. A devotional or meditation in a worship team rehearsal should be easygoing and concise. These presentations should foster interest in the things of the Lord without being overbearing, opinionated, or legalistic. They should be grace motivated by inspiring a corporate sense of hope, positivity, and "joy unspeakable, full of glory!"[15]

Over the course of a year's scheduling, I would encourage a focus on:

- worship studies from the Bible, including the "what and why"
- key biblical leaders who found solace in hard times by singing
- the four pillars of the Christian walk (Ten Commandments, three things, beatitudes, and fruit and gifts of the Spirit)
- value of the psalms in times of trouble, pain, or despair
- benefits of the New Testament words of merit: love, grace, mercy, forgiveness, and brotherly kindness
- current affairs that may need a Christian worldview application
- processing of a bad day
- biblical answers to tough questions
- importance of unity
- benefits of longevity
- noting the difference between practicing and rehearsing
- offering one's firstfruits

I selected twelve topics to illustrate that each title could represent a month's teaching in rehearsal. Some topics are theological, designed to build a proper doctrine. Others are personal, designed to reinforce character. Still others are practically designed to instill decorum.

Many preachers will spend the summer outlining the sermons for the following year of ministry. I affirm this method of planning because being systematic focuses a worship leader to look ahead and schedule enough time to invoke God's blessing, accomplish the necessary research, and write the devotional in enough time to be comfortable with the material by the night of presentation.

Someone once said that a good sermon reflects an hour's study for

---

[15] Barney Elliott Warren, "Joy Unspeakable," 1900.

each minute in the pulpit. That was certainly true for me in my formative years in morning staff devotions. Depending on the material and subject matter—even today—a new sermon could still reflect that kind of time allotment for me.

Perhaps you're reading this and wondering why. Why should I prioritize a devotional segment in my weekly rehearsal? Don't I have enough to do to prepare the songs for worship and instill a sense of vocal discipline in my singers?

The *presentation of the spirit* is an intriguing phrase of merit. To be spirit-formed is to be quickened by the power of the Holy Spirit to believe in impossibilities. This is what hearing the Word of God does in the hearts of men and women. For the Word is "sharper than a two-edged sword" (Hebrews 4:12) and knocks down fear, doubt, and unbelief. This is precisely what the body needs to perceive each time they gather.

> *At worship's core, preparation of the songs and preparation of the spirit are co-equal parts of the equation, which, on Sunday, brings a refreshing to the body.*

If the worship team is alive in a Spirit-formed mind-set, nothing is impossible! It was another mentor, Pastor Jack Hayford, who coined the phrase, *spirit-formed*, in his writings a decade ago. It is the same faith quotient that arose in Mary, upon hearing the word of her miracle, who exclaimed, "For with God, nothing shall be impossible" (Luke 1:37).

"Faith comes by hearing and hearing by the Word of God" (Romans 10:17).

It is therefore illogical to assume that a worship team can be prepared to lead people of faith in faith unless they are spirit-formed in the rehearsal modality. I believe in the bifurcation of a worship leader's skill set.

> *We must be men and women of musical mastery and Spirit-fullness.*

Without the former, we make noise, not music. How is God honored by sloppiness? Without the latter, we are but "a clanging cymbal" (1 Corinthians 13:1), void of spiritual impact. How is God honored by a mere concert void of impact?

What's more, I want to encourage worship leaders to consider the dual-lane perspective of becoming a master musician and a skilled expositor. In rehearsal, we must seriously prepare the songs and practice the spoken Word. In this way, worship team members are actualizing Paul's writing, "For it is God who, working in you to will and to act in order to fulfill His good purpose" (Philippians 2:13) as they serve the ministry of music.

By way of an example, I am including two sermons to illuminate the role of worship leader as pastor to the musical family of the church. One devotional is instructional; the other is inspirational. So as not to chunk too much material in one chapter, I will reflect on the instructional meditation first and the inspirational devotion in the next chapter.

Three Biblical Songs

A Song in Battle

- 2 Chronicles 20:20–22: Now, when they began to sing and to praise, the Lord set ambushes against the people of Ammon, Moab and Mount Seir, who had come against Judah, and they were defeated (verse 22).

On the surface, the story seems counterintuitive. An evil army is breathing down on the people of God. They are surrounded and intimidated. The king calls on the Lord. The divine directive seems risky to the human eye, but the king obeys. Essentially the plan involves singers going ahead of soldiers to worship. Can you imagine the scene? It's just extraordinary!

As the singers broke into praise, the Lord supernaturally amplified their song. Its tones reverberated across the landscape like thunder. The enemy was filled with sudden fear and committed mass suicide. Victory came to those who obeyed. The song in battle was, therefore, scripted in the Old Testament for all humanity to witness and emulate.

So here we are, thousands of years later, studying the text and articulating its outcomes. A song's potential to rally people and redeem situations is peerless. Songs are weapons. In the spirit realm, a song can crush the works of the adversary. (Oh, how I wish the leadership of the church really understood this spiritual reality.)

Alas, if this story was scripted today it might go like this. In my second year as director of music for The Church On The Way, our sanctuary choir was invited to sing for a mayor's prayer breakfast in downtown LA. We gathered early in the morning, only to find out that everything was to go wrong.

For example, we forgot to place music stands on the truck. For this occasion, I was to conduct a thirty-piece orchestra. Now it's 6:00 a.m.! Everyone is present to sound check, and there were no music stands. To make matters worse, the church campus was forty-five minutes away!

However, that was not our only hindrance. It was so hot in the auditorium that I began asking the servers about the possibility of air-conditioning. The dilemma was that I didn't speak fluent Spanish and no one understood my request.

Further, the hotel employee assigned to take us to a holding room for a continental breakfast obviously woke up on the wrong side of the bed. She ignored our pleas for "a cup of cold water" (Matthew 10:42) and was anything but hospitable. Our breakfast featured paper cups and warm water, a double hit to the solar plexus.

Finally I gathered the choir and retorted, "I'm tempted to forget why we came here today!"

All of a sudden, an alto raised her hand and responded, "Pastor, perhaps we should pray!"

I simply nodded my head.

During the prayer, another alto received a picture from the Lord. She said, "While we prayed, I saw [in the spirit] thousands of demons flying out of the windows of the hotel and into the Pacific Ocean. I believe we're going to prevail!"

Sure enough, a few minutes later we entered the auditorium. Soon we were singing the song, "Be Strong and Take Courage." It was a moving experience for all of us.

Unannounced, the mayor of Los Angeles went to the podium immediately following our song. He said, "I am wondering if the choir from Pastor Hayford's church could come to the mayor's mansion every morning and sing that song? You see, while they were singing, I lost my fear! I'm actually not afraid for the first time since being voted in as mayor! Could that choir possibly come to my home and sing that song for me each morning?"

Although we suffered frustration in the preparation of our song, our choice to pray moved the hand of God. Our song, as a weapon of faith, banished the mayor's fear, and in its place came "the peace beyond understanding" (Philippians 4:7).

You see, the song of the Lord travels through time and space with the velocity of a rocket. A song carries power to grace our weakness, soothe our pain, and cause our distress to cease. Songs minister peace in the storm, and they magnify the name of the Lord.

> *When songs are coupled with anointing, miracles still ensue.*

When a test presents itself—sing! When a trial seemingly does not end—sing! When the fire of temptation scorches—it's time to sing!

The biblical story of the song in battle was no coincidence. It happened long ago as a reminder of one of the true secrets of Kingdom life. When stressed, relief isn't necessarily in a pill. It's in a song!

The Song of Creativity[16]

- Job 38:4, 7: Where were you when I laid the earth's foundation? On what were its footing set, or who laid its cornerstone while all the angels sang?

The final chapters of the book of Job delineate a fascinating conversation between God and His servant. Job has obviously been through the ringer. Near the end of this epic trial, he begins to lose heart. So the Lord walks Job through a series of questions.

The questions rally Job's faith. He braces himself like a man (40:7) and testifies, "I know that you [God Almighty] can do all things; no plan of yours can be thwarted" (42:2). Job's life is then vindicated (42:12–17), and he lives the rest of his life in prosperity and peace.

Now watch this! Amid all the questions, the Lord mentions something

---

[16] From a sermon by Amos Dodge, preached at Capital Church, Washington, DC.

noteworthy. While rehearsing how He created the world, He mentioned that angels were singing. It's as if He is saying to Job, "Look, you sing, and I'll create!"

In other words, God is testifying, "I can do anything, Job! But I do My best work when those who love Me sing. Sing to Me, and I'll amaze you with what I will do!"

This insight into the conversation between God and Job has revolutionized my perspective about creative impartation. I believe if we will sing to the Lord while we serve, He'll assist us in supernatural ways. We can do so much more by grace than we could ever do on our own. Singing unlocks a door to the supernatural and His infinite creativity.

What does this mean for you and me? The power of a gospel song is limitless. That is what this passage of scripture indicates. In the singing of a song, God Almighty is honored. He then becomes attentive to the needs of His people as He hears them worship Him in all the seasons of their lives, though few actually actualize the inherent truth of this promise. It is easy to praise the Lord when we are happy and secure. It is a sacrifice to sing when we are tempted and tried. The greatest opportunity before us as worship leaders may be found in the moment when we are trying to create something artistic and find ourselves painted into a corner.

Creating art is infinitely complex. For example, when composing a song, a composer usually begins with a catchy theme, a phrase, or melodic motif. Next, he or she writes a response that becomes a second phrase that somehow balances the first musical idea on paper. The chorus or refrain of the song will take additional music that complements the compositional style of the verse. Then there is the contrasting music needed for the bridge, and a great song must have potent lyrics. Finally a winning lyric always has a hook. The hook is a distinctive phrase that is easy to sing and, more importantly, easy to remember.

> *Writing a melodic motif is only the beginning of a long, creative journey.*

In a burst of creativity, our scriptural text is telling us to go counterintuitive. The Lord basically told Job to sing! Singing involves the welcoming of the Holy Spirit to inspire ideas, concepts, and artistic creation from deep within our spirit. It works!

The great songs of praise and worship were facilitated through divine inspiration. Composers drew near to God, and God drew near to them (James 4:8). Songs are little masterpieces that remind us that God is the master musician. If He is in the middle of our creativity, our songs will find a place in a congregation's worship lexicon and open doors, spark original ideas, and bind the works of the adversary.

The Job narrative makes this clear. Sing, Job, and I'll do My best work when you sing!

What is it about a song that God loves? I submit there are four qualities to which God responds.

The Elements+ of a Song Are Pleasing

Songs have melody, harmony, and rhythm. They exist in a form or architecture, if you will. When these traits of composition are carefully balanced and creatively designed with the poetry of a lyric, this pleases our Lord and stimulates His munificence. When the beauty of a song enriches both head and heart, the result is indeed compelling.

I commuted to California some years ago to rehearse a Christmas choir and then served for almost a year as a guest worship leader. One day, my flight was full of little children who were misbehaving. Amid the chaos, I reached for my iPod and instantly accessed the presence of the Lord through song. In a matter of an hour, my creativity flourished. By the time the plane landed in LA, I had outlined two lectures, developed a rehearsal plan, wrote an order of worship, and settled on a series of ideas for an upcoming proposal. On the surface, the children were annoyingly distracting, but when the music began, my focus shifted. Amid my worship of the Lord, creative designs flooded my mind.

The Properties of a Song Are Engaging

Songs communicate emotions and feelings. In many ways, songs are a more efficient mode of communication than prose. Songs enhance dialogue and create an atmosphere for the transformation of negative emotions to morph into positive ones. This ironic consequence is worth drilling down a bit. For example, a song can relax or energize. A song can evoke reflection or encourage perseverance. A song can reinforce a scriptural promise. A song can also provide a healthy way of escape or solidify a prophecy recently shared. In short, songs edify! John O'Donohoe aptly wrote, "Music is what language and poetry would be if they could choose."

The Dimensions of a Song Are Invigorating

Songs of praise and worship also invoke spiritual dimensions that obliterate our propensity toward amnesia. All of us tend to forget that Jesus has been remarkable in helping us live above the fray. In the moment of stress, we easily experience tunnel vision. We'll wonder, "Where are You, Lord? Why is this new trial so painful?" Then a song will be sung in church, and suddenly it occurs to us that He has been faithful in the past. If we can recapture His grandeur and not dwell on the size of our problem, He'll lift the burden again and again!

The spirit of praise changes the way believers manage the stress of hardship. That is why seekers need to attend church with regularity. Songs remind us that He is greater than any problem, no weapon formed against us will prosper, and He is the God who heals.

What's more, we remember the scripture better when attached to a song. Songs instantaneously take us back to moments in our lives when God was faithful and will be faithful again. Once we remember how a former crisis was effectively mediated, we are built up in the inner man with faith to realize His character does not change. If He helped us before, He will help us now in our present situation. The past is definitely a prologue with God.

The Implications of a Song Are Life-giving

Bernard Kelly writes, "The apprehension of beauty awakens the deeper, more searching activity of the mind." To an unbeliever, a gospel song can awaken the truth of the Gospel. To the believer, a gospel song can deepen the truth of the Gospel.

Songs transmit life. Songs inspire creativity. Songs invigorate spirituality and foster miracles! Isaiah writes, "Sing, O barren woman!" (Isaiah 54:1). Songs can even open the door of parenthood. Is it any wonder the Lord loves to hear of songs of praise? When you and I need an idea or a way to solve a personality clash, let's choose to sing before we serve. Join me?

Songs in the Night

- Job 35:10: Who gives songs in the night.

Finally we turn to the third biblical song to find great comfort when it is dark all around. In Job 35:10, we find six words chock full of astonishing help and hope. Clearly Job needed a way to soothe the anxieties of his (pardon my pun) *night*life.

What is it about going through "a storm" at night? Why do the challenges of life and ministry appear so much gloomier at night? What about the darkness itself? Isn't it ironic that so much evil occurs after dark?

Robbers propagate, shootings proliferate, and the voice of the adversary promulgates at night. In the spirit realm, the adversary frequently attempts to steal our joy, fire evil darts, and spread fear-prone taunts at *night*. The *night* season is spiritually power-packed. Hence, my appreciation for the six simple words in our text. Job learned that singing quells *nighttime* stress. What a gift this concept is for us today.

The Bible is full of stories of *nighttime* stress and God's remedy for relief. David soothed the demonic oppression of King Saul by playing songs skillfully during his "dark *night* of the soul." Paul and Silas sang at midnight and achieved an amazing prison breakthrough.

Saints too have put this practice to work. Corrie ten Boom, a beloved heroine of WWII, and her younger sister, Betsy, battled after dark in a German prisoner of war camp. As Betsy was growing ever weaker, she once asked Corrie why she wanted to sing with such fervor at *night*. Corrie replied, "At night we sing our songs, and our songs give us courage."

Slaves sang beautiful spirituals in their cabins after dark as well. Their songs not only bolstered their spirits during that dark, dank period in American history but also inspired a new genre of American art, jazz.

The concept of beauty emanating from smoldering ash is noteworthy. It has been said, "Even in misfortune there are seeds of great fortune." The hymn writer would pen,

Some through the water

Some through the flood,

Some through the fire

But all through the blood.

Some through great sorrow

But God gives a song,

In the night season

And all the day long.[17]

In analyzing the ebb and flow of nature, there is an axiom that states, "No storm, even a stage five hurricane, lasts forever." So it is with a nighttime spiritual attack. No nighttime attack lasts forever. Soon the dawn cracks the blackened sky, and the sun rises again in the east!

I am thankful, however, that amid a nighttime assail there is a way to access comfort. Sing a song! Offer the song as a sacrifice of praise. The result will summon our faith and dispel our fear. Longfellow would confirm,

Let the night be filled with music

And the cares that infest the day

Will fold their tents ...

And, as silently, steal away.

These three biblical songs from the Old Testament serve as examples for us today in the service of the church. Just because we're leaders in worship does not exempt us from the trials and temptations of life.

---

[17] George A. Moore, *God Leads His Dear Children.*

However, there is a promise from the Word of God that states, "You are my hiding place; You will protect me from trouble and surround me with songs of deliverance" (2 Samuel 22:31). This I believe.

Two concepts are on our table today at worship's core: devotions and songs of deliverance matter!

There are times in the life of a worship team when anxiety mounts. There are also times when shock from a sudden calamity overwhelms and tempts us to be discouraged, moments when illness strikes like a thief in the night. In these tenuous moments, a worship leader has a choice. The trouble can be addressed through a devotional or an extended worship experience like singing to the Lord the song of deliverance right there in the rehearsal or maybe through partaking in the Holy Communion.

I was forty-one years old before I clearly understood the value of taking the Holy Communion outside of a church service. I was visiting Dr. Hayford one afternoon in his private office when all of a sudden, he stopped and asked how my wife was feeling. At the time, she was pregnant with our third son and had developed a painful case of bursitis in her shoulder.

I told him about her pain, and he quipped, "Have you taken the Holy Communion in your home, Tom?"

I was instantly confused and asked in skepticism, "I never knew that was a possibility, Pastor."

Immediately he told me to have his assistant clear his evening schedule and invite another couple to join us. He said that he and his wife would come to our house after dinner to pray and serve Holy Communion. The six of us gathered in our living room and began to pray. Then Dr. Hayford served the elements. He modeled a life lesson that evening that we have never forgotten. My lovely wife was healed, and she went through the rest of the pregnancy free from discomfort in that arm.

From a perspective that spans four decades, I can honestly say bringing the Lord into the rehearsal works!

I have come to believe in the mighty power of taking Holy Communion when my family or my church ensembles

127

need an extraordinary intervention from the Lord. Some of the most intimate times of my ministry with choirs, worship teams, and family members have occurred when we have sung the songs of deliverance and welcomed the manifest presence of the Lord while receiving Holy Communion.

One of the ways we know "God is still working in us" (Philippians 1:6) is when we celebrate Holy Communion in times of trouble. When we welcome His presence through prayer, song, and partaking of Holy Communion, His hand is free to heal and deliver.

Seeds from the Core

1. Worship leaders have to develop a multifactorial skill set. They must be excellent musicians, competent administrators, and clear-headed public speakers capable of bringing a cogent word from the Lord to the rehearsal.
2. Devotions edify the workers and remind us just how able the Lord is.
3. From the Old Testament, three songs helped the people of Israel dominate their environment when they needed help.
4. The song of creativity is especially meaningful if worship leaders can apply its merit by faith.

A word spoken at the right time is like fruit of gold set in silver.

—Proverbs 25:11

CHAPTER 9

NOW BRING ME A MUSICIAN

Speaking to my choirs and worship teams about the things of the Lord has been one of the most satisfying experiences of my ministerial life. Looking back, I have been blessed beyond measure. I've conducted holiday music in symphony halls and at the Pentagon in Washington, DC. I've addressed worship leaders in national conferences and consulted denominational executives. My Baltimore choir was even invited to sing for the inauguration of a US president.

All of those accolades notwithstanding, my greatest work has been in much smaller rooms of singers reflecting on a verse of scripture before a concert or worship service. There is something sublime about the psychological principle of flow in educational parlance or the anointing in theological parlance, which begins to capture everyone's attention in rehearsal until we want to take off our shoes, for suddenly the ground beneath us seems holy. Once the team comes into agreement and offers their artistry as "a living sacrifice," watch out (Romans 12:1)!

That divine sense of purpose unlocks God's blessing. It is as if the hand of God has descended as with the prophets of old. Empowered by His touch, the singers and players can step before a sanctuary in godly confidence to offer praise and worship.

In that rarified air of spiritual dynamism, nature, the cosmos, and heaven itself are called to attention as we give homage to the Creator, shout His praise in Zion, and call the earth to thunder for joy. And the trees burst forth in color, as Jesus, the King of Kings and Lord of Lords, has been invited to enter the singing sanctuary.

I discovered that the mystery of preparing voices to lead worship is found in the well-prepared spoken word delivered prior to an event. This word is the rehearsal devotional.

> *On the wings of a song, His presence is sensed, and the church becomes holy ground with "peace like a river attending my way!"*[16]

If I prepare correctly, putting due diligence into my early rise before His Majesty, He always inspires what I should say. This discovery of learning how to motivate the laity in Christian service and spiritual foundation in this communion is among the most important keys to the Kingdom I have ever uncovered.

Clearly, a well-conceived meditation positively impacts our capacity to focus on the things of God. Focus informs a corporate unity. Unity, in turn, releases an anointing, and in the twinkling of an eye, congregants, clergy, and choristers are undeniably caught up in His holy presence where scripture proclaims, "there is a fullness of joy" (Psalm 16:11).

> *If the members are properly focused before an event, unified by a word "aptly spoken," they can achieve spiritual acts of courage that defy their individual musical prowess.*

Such was the day when I first spoke the following teaching about one of the most incredible ironies in holy writ. The devotional before us is found in the Old Testament book of 2 Kings 3:3–18. Here is the story in a nutshell.

The people of Israel were always facing some kind of battle from an enemy host. That fact is comforting to me. In fact, I once heard a speaker quip, "In life it seems like we are either in a trial, coming out of a trial, or getting ready for the next trial!"

The former king of Israel, Ahab, had a business deal with the king of Moab. When Ahab died, the king of Moab reneged on the deal with Jehoram, Ahab's son, the new king of Israel. Word of this breakdown quickly spread throughout the region. Two other kings came to Jehoram's defense, and together they devised a plan to overtake the Moab army over this broken business contract.

---

[18] Horatio Spatford, "It Is Well with My Soul," 1873.

Jehoram asked the kings of Samaria and Judah, "Which way shall we go to invade the territory of Moab?" Unfortunately they elected to go around the edge of the country rather than straight through (which would have saved time and treasure). The journey around the edge of the country became a seven-day march.

Along the way, chaos broke loose! They ran out of water. How could they possibly engage the well-seasoned Moab army without sustenance?

The Word Explored

Verse	Action
10	The kings bemoan: Has the Lord brought us this far to hand us over to the enemy now?
11	Judah's king asks, "Isn't there a prophet around here somewhere? Maybe he can get us out of this mess."
12	The three kings suspend the journey to hunt for the prophet, Elisha, who had become frustrated with their poor planning.
13–14	Elisha dismisses their interruption with sarcasm. Jehoram pleads for mercy. Elisha retorts, "If it were not for your Father, sir, I would dismiss you forthwith. Now, bring me a musician!"
15–18	Please read carefully as the Bible records, "When the musician played, the hand of the Lord came upon Elisha."

In times of conflict, leaders have to move decisively. This was the case on that momentous afternoon in the desert. Amid the toxicity, Elisha summoned a skillful musician, perhaps the true unsung hero of this little debacle, to play as he prayed. The end result was life-changing.

Music moved the hand of God. Is there any sentence in the entire Bible that would confirm our call to ministry more profoundly?

The ability of a song to create a reverent atmosphere, to silence our fears and the adversary's lies, is peerless. When a gospel song is sung, chaos is quelled, the rattling sense of urgency subsides, and the people of God can freely exhale.

Could that have been in David's heart when he wrote, "You prepare a table before me in the presence of my enemies" (Psalm 23:5)?

Two Words Explained

"When the musician played, the hand of the Lord came upon Elisha" (2 Kings 3:15). This linchpin scripture requires one more look. Beyond the cause and effect of the music being played and the hand of the Lord being moved, can you perceive the why? There are strategic implications from the original language that we cannot gloss over in our desire to internalize this story's meaning.

At worship's core, there is a principle to learn and a process to entreat by noting the linguistic inferences of the terms:

- *A Musician:* noting what scholars have researched about his advanced musical skill, personal devotion, and aptitude to perceive the moment
- *The Hand of God:* a phrase that theologians agree is used over a thousand times in the scriptures to underscore God's acts and actions on our behalf

Elisha, according to Matthew Henry, "was ruffled by the encounter with Jehoram."[19] The young king had dabbled with the gods of Baal, and although the statues were removed, he maintained a friendship with the

---

[19] "Verse-by-Verse Bible Commentary, 2 Kings 3:15," https://www.studylight.org/commentary/2-kings/3-15.html.

priests of Baal. Moreover, the prophet was "irritated by the poor planning" of this dubious threesome in addition to their "shallow faith" in Jehovah.

It is important to note that before Elisha could righteously call on God to redeem this sketchy situation, he needed to be in the right frame to speak to and to hear from God. Music was the first step. His intuition in that regard was spot on. Like counting from one to ten before reacting in an anger-prone moment, the prophet bows his knee.

John Wesley writes, "All hurry of spirit and all turbulent passions, make us unfit for divine visitations."[20] The harpist kept the environment "serene." Adam Clarke then concludes, "As the music played, the power of God descended upon Elisha. This effect of music was generally acknowledged in every civilized nation."[21]

My research strongly concludes that the musician was not only properly trained in the performance practice of the harp, but in theology as well. This was the necessary if subtle second step. The minstrel knew how to present himself before God and the prophet.

In the work of ministry, musical mastery is equally important to the possession of a humble, contrite heart before the Lord. Performance practice and ministry mindedness each carry weight. The harpist was dually qualified. Consequently he became a conduit for impartation.

Biblical truth is timeless. What is important for us to glean from this passage of scripture is not just that the minstrel played with distinction, but that he came into the situation knowing how to minister to the Lord. That is a very different issue from musical talent. The psalmist David often wrote about maintaining a clean heart before the Lord (Psalm 51:10). Keeping our heart pure by applying the daily disciplines of repentance, forgiveness and self-control seem to be a universally accepted starting point. A worship leader who has a short memory of those who have been hurtful and a very large capacity to show patience toward one's enemies may find the hand of God readily present to guard and guide.

Now to the second concept, the hand of God. In this context, Wesley writes, "The hand of God refers to the spirit of prophecy. It is important to

---

[20] Ibid.

[21] Ibid.

note the ability to prophesy was not a natural or acquired virtue inherent in Elisha, but a singular gift of God given to whom and when He pleased."[22]

"Revelation is seldom given to those who are merely curious," notes Pastor Bill Johnson. Prophecy or revelation is given to those who have proven character and a track record of honoring the Lord. Elisha was just this kind of believer. As he prayed, God's hand came upon him.

I believe the hand of God signifies the benevolent activity of God on our behalf. According to experts, the hand of God, "Created the world, holds the world in place, inspired the prophets, protects the people of God, redeems the people of God, ensures our success as the people of God, fulfills the purposes of God, and symbolizes the power of God."[23]

The phrase, "the hand of God," can be observed in some of the most beautiful promises in the entire Bible.

- "Fear not, for I am with you. Be not dismayed for I am your God; I will strengthen you. I will help you; I will uphold you with my righteous right hand" (Isaiah 41:10).
- "My soul clings to you; your right hand upholds me" (Psalm 63:8).
- "The hand of our God is for good on all who seek Him" (Ezra 8:21).
- "Behold, the Lord's hand is not shortened, that it cannot save, or his ear, that it cannot hear" (Isaiah 59:1).
- "Jabez cried out to the God of Israel, 'Oh that you would bless me and enlarge my territory! Let your hand be with me, and keep me from harm so that I will be free from pain'" (1 Chronicles 4:10).
- "The word of the Lord came to Ezekiel, the priest, in the land of the Chaldeans, and the hand of the Lord was upon him there" (Ezekiel 1:3).
- "Then I said to them, 'You see the trouble we are in, how Jerusalem lies in ruins with its gates burned. Come, let us build the wall of Jerusalem, that we may no longer suffer derision.' And I told them of the hand of my God that had been upon me for good, and also of the words the king had spoken to me. And they said, 'Let us

---

[22] Ibid.
[23] "Hand," https://www.biblestudytools.com/dictionary/hand.

rise up and build,' so they strengthened their hands for the good work" (Nehemiah 2:17–18).

- "And Jesus reached out his hand and touched the man. 'I am willing,' he said. 'Be clean!' And immediately he was cleansed of his leprosy" (Matthew 8:3).

As with Elisha who quieted his spirit while the harpist played, let us learn the valuable lesson from this text and live the kind of life that pleases the Lord. That way we can be assured that the hand of the Lord will move on our behalf as well.

The Word Applied

When confused by life's unexpected surprises, listening to a song is always the right thing to do. Elisha did. If we can move in the same anointing as the harpist of old, our audience may find the answers for which they are searching. Ask the worship team:

- Who among our team has just been blindsided by a bad report or vicious attack?
- Who is facing a hard choice, not knowing where to turn?
- Who needs a breakthrough and needs it now?
- In spite of your troubles, you have come to minister to others. I am here to say that you did the right thing. Before we care for the congregation, I want to give place for the Holy Spirit to care for you.
- Pray for the musicians prior to their entering the sanctuary.

When humbled by poor planning and facing sure defeat, the hapless kings amazingly did the right thing. They asked for help from the prophet. In effect, they went to church!

As a sidebar, I cannot help but state the obvious. The strategic use of a musician's gift to incite a miracle plan while the enemy army was sensing an easy victory is a

> *I believe in filling the cup of the volunteer musicians before asking them to pour themselves into the needs of the congregation.*

timeless description of hell's overreach. We can take heart in reading this story, for under pressure the saints always have a proven "way of escape" (1 Corinthians 10:13)! We can pray and sing a song of deliverance.

Music is often God's secret weapon. When a song is properly presented, the enemy's minions have to flee, and relief replaces anxiety. This epic story in 2 Kings 3 has been handed down from generation to generation for all to appreciate. This story told in a devotional format can electrify a room of musicians.

It can help the worship team see their purpose in a fresh way. It can raise the bar of commitment and inspire a new passion for ministry. It can bolster the team's faith, renew their vision, and infuse a sense of the divine in their practical efforts to effectively share compassion with a hurting congregation through song.

Frankly, this story almost preaches itself. We just have to be studious enough to research the gems from the original language and master the art of preaching by which we bring the gems of scripture to light.

Bringing this chapter to a close, I am reminded of the enduring words of the apostle Paul in 2 Timothy 2:15. "Do your best to present yourself to God as one approved, a worker who does not need to be ashamed and who correctly handles the word of truth."

Seeds from the Core

1. Devotions matter. Properly communicated, they motivate spiritual commitment and build faith to minister to the people in song.
2. The truth in 2 Kings 3 has merit in a worship team context. Study this passage with care and concern.
3. "And when the musician played, the hand of God came upon Elisha." May it fall on us as well!
4. God's ways are higher than ours. We must seek His help. We must rely on His ingenuity, not our own. We must also stay humble and utterly dependent on His guidance when presenting devotionals in the rehearsal context.

Then the Grinch thought of something he hadn't before.
What if Christmas, he thought, doesn't come from a store?
What if Christmas, perhaps, means a little bit more.

—Dr. Seuss

CHAPTER 10

AN ORANGE CHRISTMAS

It was an icy cold December morning in 1932. My father was five years old. All he wanted for Christmas that year was a bicycle. Instead, all he received was an orange. The Depression of the thirties hit the Midwest of my country hard. Farms were closing by the bushel full. Ours was no exception. So my loving grandparents did the best they could. They gave their little boy all they could give, a piece of fruit.

This Christmas I placed an orange on the coffee table in our living room, and amid the splendor of sharing gifts with our three sons, I paused to share the story. Our sons, all grown now, were shocked. My comments were succinct and simple. Everyone's eyes filled up. I never heard my father complain about that meager gift or his parents whom he clearly understood, in retrospect, were nearly destitute. Rather my dad's memories focused on the bike he did receive four years later.

I always respected my father's gracious demeanor when speaking of his parents. I experienced them as industrious, godly, and loving. I was saddened by the loss of their farm but greatly encouraged by their stories of resiliency as they dusted off and started over. They were irrepressible. To this day, when the Christmas season arrives, there comes a day when momentarily I will reflect on my grandparents' orange Christmas. In that moment, yuletide takes on a deeper dimension.

Although my wife and I have been able to provide lovely Christmases for our sons, I nonetheless look for ways to give something back during this holy, multicultural, complex time of year. At Christmastime, emotions run high. People create expectations that may be implausible. Others search

141

for love in wrong places. All in all, without Christ, Christmas can be an emotionally charged proposition.

Maybe that is why presenting a holiday concert, not only for my church but for the greater community at large, was such an integral part of my pastoral ministry. My father's early Christmas disappointment informed my intentionality to help others find hope and peace at the holidays. If people from our circle of influence could find the real meaning of Christmas in a concert setting without a heavy guilt trip, I believed their lives would be enhanced.

At worship's core, Christmas is a prime opportunity to dramatically witness Jesus to the community at large through festive, joyous, and expressive music. Unfortunately the joy of a special community outreach at Christmastime is largely overlooked these days in lieu of contemporary Christian models for delivering holiday repertoire. The great choirs of my generation have been replaced by rock bands and light shows.

Although there is a place in our churches for modernity, I see an ironic consequence. While the music of worship appeals to those inside the church, a trend to secularize Christmas outside the church is growing. It appears as though the witness of the church has essentially been stifled if not snuffed out entirely. Fewer choirs sing, "O come, let us adore Him." Instead the culture takes Christmas advice from the media or the movies.

Put simply, in this last chapter of my book I am taking a bold stance. I believe in a different paradigm for the building of the church in terms of how we address the Christmas holidays. Christmas is simply too important and too ripe for evangelism to hide under a bushel.

Hollywood and Bollywood know that. 5th Avenue in New York City knows that too. Billions of dollars are exchanged trying to rekindle the mystic feeling of Christmas once again. We know the truth! We must "let the truth set us free" (John 8:32). We should be free to share the truth of Christmas in musical splendor with those who are still in darkness.

Jesus was born in a humble setting to say, "Peace on earth, good will toward men" (Luke 2:14)! Angels sang. Wise men journeyed. Shepherds rejoiced. Mary and Joseph courageously stepped up to the plate to fulfill their destiny.

These bullet statements are bursting with theology, hope, and harvest potential. Yet the reality is, if the church is silent or worse, insular at

Christmas, secular culture will pervert the occasion for mere financial gain.

This is terribly unfortunate. Too many people are hurting and searching while we gather to worship the newborn King. I believe we should be bold and extravagant in our witness at the holiday season. There is simply no end to the creative possibilities. Therefore, I will present a discussion about how to witness at Christmastime within the genre of a worship team and a reestablished choir. I will also offer a strategy in terms of building a lasting ministry of music, from simple to sophisticated. I am presenting a proposal entitled "An Orange Christmas."

I chose to entitle this chapter *An Orange Christmas* for two essential, yet contrasting, reasons. An Orange Christmas refers not only to my father's humble gift but to the fruit's bright color, which normally does not find its way into the Christmas decorating palette.

Orange can bring feelings of joy, excitement, and enthusiasm to the season! As the church, our answer is "orange." An orange strategy opens the door widely to the hurting and disenfranchised in the community and points to the wonder-working power of the Living Christ to the entire world with healing in His hands.

Let's refer to this new ministry opportunity as *Code Orange.* Code Orange will become an annual evangelistic opportunity to present the Christ of Christmas as our Lord and Savior through musical excellence because only Jesus can put lives back together, heal one's memory, restore one's health, redeem one's mistakes, forgive one's sins, and bring purpose to one's existence.

Use the information provided below to celebrate the truth of the Luke accounting in a colorful, musical, and inviting an orange concert offering to all within your church's area of influence.

The Four Phases of Music Ministry

There are four distinct seasons of ministry in a church department of music. Each phase has a different level of administrative challenge. Each carries an increasing responsibility for musical proficiency and calendar facilitation. Each requires increasing flexibility, creativity, accountability, and spirituality.

The ministry criterion for church or departmental growth always begins with an individual leader. Truthfully, the size of a ministry more often than not reflects both a leader's overall capacity for growth and a tireless work ethic. Sadly, over my decades in the seminary classroom, I have found a limited number of ministers willing to pay the price.

Many leaders are bright but lazy. Others have a great love for people but shy away from developing good study habits or lifelong learning skills. Still, more have personal challenges—be it physical, emotional, or spiritual—that countermand their effectiveness over time. The parable of the talents comes to mind here. Of course the parable is not about competition with the ministerium at large, but within us individually.

> *Given who God made each of us to be, in the final analysis, we all will answer for the ways in which we developed our innate skill set, our individual gift mix.*

Building a Worship Team

In the opening days of a new church, a worship leader will have to initiate several systems. First, a decision will need to be made about whether to audition or interview the singers and players.

An interview is a meeting in which one assesses a musician's relative ability to be a part of a team. The interviewer will ask salient questions in such a way as to try to determine if the potential singer or player will accept responsibility for arriving on time, remaining on task throughout the rehearsal, and becoming servant-minded.

What you are looking for are responsible musicians who will naturally see a need and fill it. Preferably, a worship team member will be proactive in cultivating harmony in the atmosphere around them. Ideally, they should go out of their way to make others welcome, comfortable, and wanted. These attributes are essential qualities of an effective, unified worship team. Developing a questionnaire with different scenarios can help an interviewer guide the discussion toward determining if these qualities are in the potential candidate.

An audition is principally a process by which one assesses an individual's musical aptitude. I opt to interview because spiritual gifting outweighs the musical imperfections in the beginning. One caveat: Each singer chosen to serve must be able to match pitch.

Second, materials and rehearsal space are needed. Where will the worship team convene? Rehearse? Is there a piano there? How will the worship team master music? Will the music be taught by rote? Will there be printed lead sheets or hymn tunes to read? Is there a place for the group to store a folder, a pencil, and a Bible? Is there a place for refreshment storage? Is the room comfortable, inviting, and soothing?

Additionally a telephone tree or an email contact list should be organized so the ensemble can communicate with each other for quick announcements, assistance, or prayer requests. Who will clean the room? Who will set the temperature? Who will brew the drinks? Who will pray ahead of a rehearsal? Who will keep track of the sick or bereaved? Who will plan fellowship times? Who will coordinate travel arrangements should the worship team agree to present music for another church or community event?

Finally, a set of teachings will need to be shared early in the ministry. To that end, perhaps the most important understanding is the clear differentiation between acting like a volunteer versus serving the ministry with integrity.

I personally believe God calls every believer to missional work. I am not necessarily saying that the call to serve is vocational. Rather I believe that all Christians have purpose and gifting. When a seeker finds Jesus and becomes aware of "how fearfully and wonderfully they have been made," there flashes in an individual's spirit a desire to serve others (Psalm 139:14).

This service could be a thousand different things. The issue is not in what capacity an individual serves, but how the service is rendered. Are we nonchalant or serious? Do we serve to find fault or solutions to the presenting challenges a church encounters on a weekly basis? In short, is our attitude a help or a hindrance?

> *A ministry will flounder at the hand of the volunteer mind-set but flourish if individuals will make the commitment to serve the Lord with all their might.*

A. W. Tozer said, "To serve God does not narrow one's life; rather it brings it to the level of highest possible fulfillment." Tozer's clarification is precisely what I have experienced throughout my life with volunteers in the two ministry settings in which I served.

When I start a new ministry, I recruit. I interview. I welcome possible candidates enthusiastically. Ultimately I organize a day of orientation where we speak as a team about the value of praise and worship and outline music education parameters to those who have little experience singing so they will feel more comfortable with the musical elements of being on a worship team. Then I will delve into the process of becoming a servant.

We will discuss the differences between acting like a volunteer versus actualizing a call to serve. We will review biblical lists for interacting with fellow believers in a redemptive way. We will discuss how important it is to function with ethical purity in the body of Christ.

For a clearer understanding of the difference between a volunteer mindset or a called-of-God mindset, please internalize the following chart:

Volunteer	Called
Carefree	Careful
Lacks focus	Clearly focused
Casual about time	Prompt
Easily distracted	On task
Undependable	Dependable
Oblivious to the needs in the room	Sees problems before they manifest
Problem maker	Problem solver
Quits if stressed	Taps the inner strength to press on
Absents are high	Commitment is high
Comes to the rehearsal musically unprepared	Comes to the rehearsal prepared
Can be a gossip	Holds confidences at all cost

If the distinction is unmistakable from the start, the ministry of music will be established on solid ground—dare I say holy ground. For other notable devotional presentations, please go to appendix 3.

Code Orange Alert!

With regard to presenting a Christmas event with a newly formed worship team, "do not despise the day of a small beginning" (Zechariah 4:10). There is elegance in simplicity. The point of a church's first Christmas concert is to provide an opportunity for the church family's circle of influence to attend an event that is safe and comfortable entertaining. A Christmas concert is a hook, an introduction. It should feel like a recital, not another church service. The words spoken should be conversational, not liturgical.

Motivational speaker John Maxwell once wrote, "Show them how much you care before showing them how much you know." Creating a vibe for a Christmas concert starts with an understanding of Maxwell's axiom. Be friendly, not religious in tone. Let the music speak. Let the essence of Christmas shine! Let the message be about Jesus, not church membership. Offer no pressure, no hype!

This is a seeker event. Observe concert protocols. Decorate the space with color and candles. Sing familiar carols. Unison singing is perfectly acceptable—at first. Dress in holiday colors. Consider using a narrator in between selections or have a credible young person recite a poem. Perhaps add a soloist to the program. Possibly use a guest instrumentalist to flavor the concert with an additional element of musical variety.

Finally keep the event relatively short. Close with a pastoral invitation. Serve some light refreshments if possible. You'll be utterly delighted with the response!

Growing a Choir

As the church grows, more congregants will want to join the music ministry. I believe in any congregation of maturing believers, 10 percent have the gift of music. This statistic is not born out of research methodology. Rather it is a finding of mine based on personal experience. It is, therefore, incumbent on the leadership of the church to provide a platform for those who are musically inclined to use their gifts in service of the King. Opening up the ministry to new participants is a process that must be saturated in prayer.

Twice yearly, I would evaluate my ministry before the Lord in prayer and solitude. Often my prayers would go something like, "Lord, am I doing my best? Could I improve? Please guide me. For I want to be counted worthy. I want to be a man who stands before You, Lord, having used all the gifts and talents to the best of my ability."

In July of each year, I would recruit new members. The following January we would announce new programmatic decisions and designs. In American churches, we generally follow the school year in terms of introducing new programs in the fall and announcing yearly themes in January. Because our younger families live by the academic calendar—September to June—our churches find that the fall is an ideal time to welcome new musicians, the winter brings new mission opportunities, and the spring focuses on discipleship. That leaves the summer as a time to retool, relax, evaluate, and contemplate.

In my consulting, I am frequently asked by pastors who are experiencing growth in a church plant when they should start a choir. Interestingly, the average size of a church choir is sixteen voices. That means it is entirely possible to field a Christmas choir, in addition to experiencing a fine worship team, in a relatively short amount of time.

This is an important step forward for the ministry. Once the church can bifurcate with an emphasis on worship and an emphasis on choral performance practice, the ministry is on the verge of rapid growth. You see, a choir can be a worship team, but a worship team cannot be a choir.

Worship teams exist to bring modern songs in simple harmony before the body in contemporary genre in order to bless the Lord and include the youth in adult service formats. That idea is in and of itself a noble objective. The premise of contemporary Christian music enjoys worldwide approval. It is the overwhelming trend of our time. That being said, there is still a useful place for depth and variety in a contemporary church worship repertoire.

By virtue of medical advances, most congregations are blessed with three or four generations attending weekly services. By incorporating the dual opportunity of a worship team and a choir, the effectiveness of the ministry is significantly enhanced. Parents and grandparents can find refreshing in hearing the songs that ministered grace when they experienced trials decades earlier, while the youth can resonate with the contemporary songs sung at the time of their more recent born-again encounter. Each generational memory is precious. The gift of eclecticism enhances each congregant.

Put simply, I believe it is God's best to incorporate the widest style continuum possible as a local church experiences growth. Clearly the more choirs and ensembles the church can platform, the more opportunities exist for people to participate. Thereby, more generations can experience satisfaction, not alienation, when attending church. The renowned organist, Mark Thallender, said it best. Church music programs should "broaden without eliminating."

I love the contemporaneous feel of a worship team and the wealth of a choir's vast repertoire. More specifically, I love a choir's raw thunder on high holy days! I love their tender, soft touch during an altar call or following a pastoral prayer. I love, from a pastoral perspective, how many more people can find a place of ministry in a choir as compared to a worship team's need for tight harmony.

Why, you ask, do you have such passion for a choral program? To begin, choirs can sing in harmony. In fact, they have the capacity to sing a capella. Music has been written for the choral ensemble from the time of the Old Testament. A well-trained choir can bring a rich texture of historic beauty to the worship context, utterly complementing the more focused jazz and R&B gospel sound of the worship team.

Besides, the vast majority of Christmas repertoire was composed for the harmonics of a choir (SATB). So it stands to reason that using a holiday choir at Christmas and Easter makes sense. Beyond those considerations, choirs are a regular feature of symphony orchestra concerts, high school and college commencement services, military ceremonies, and governmental observances. Choirs bring a substantial presence—a dignity and aesthetic charm if you will—to an important occasion.

All across the world, in high church and free church, choirs have graced the spoken Word for centuries. A ministry will flourish with the careful organization and development of a choral program.

Now there are some interesting challenges if one has the courage to move in this direction. Choirs presuppose extra organization. Choirs require more space to house equipment, supplies, and attire. Following is a simple listing, charting some of the contrasts between administering a worship team and effectuating the development of a choir:

Worship Team	Choir
Smaller constituency	Larger community
Easy to notify	More challenging to notify
Easy to manage in rehearsal	Classroom management skills needed
Auditions required (year three onward)	Simple interviews usually suffice
Simple charts are sufficient	Printed arrangements are needed
Inexpensive budget	Larger budget
Sing in limited genres	Sing in multiple genres
Lead congregational singing	Can sing in a variety of service slots
Leader may be inexperienced	Conducting and admin. skills required
Band members may be beginners (play by ear)	Note reading skills mandatory
Simple room is satisfactory	Risers, chairs, piano needed

A growing music ministry should develop multiple ensembles who live by the same rules and ethics under the same steeple, but function with complementary, not competitive, mission statements. Out of an eclectic arts mind-set, seeds are sown to become a multicultural city church.

Personally, my overarching regret in observing the vast paradigmatic shift from traditional to contemporary worship is that our leadership unwittingly threw the baby out with the bathwater. All over the world, we fired the choir, hurt the constituency, and limited the opportunity for musical members to ever again volunteer. That trifecta of cause and effect has borne poisonous fruit. The church has essentially become irrelevant at Christmastime. This simply should not be. I believe this shortsighted trend will morph in the days ahead. I hope cooler heads will prevail and a new generation of pastors will find the discernment to reinstate the choir for the sake of the Gospel and the Kingdom so souls are saved.

Code Orange Alert!

The kind of Christmas concert one can program with a burgeoning choir and a seasoned worship team is exciting to consider. Frankly the possibilities are endless. Please examine the suggestions presented in appendix 4.

Once a choir is present, I promise you the holiday audience will double. Excitement proliferates and the reach to the community will become expansive.

Maturing a Music Ministry

The matter of maturing an arts ministry is a serious conversation. Many churches plateau; others stay relatively small for the cost of growth is large. Growth presupposes a congregational passion for the hurting and lost. Many congregants are self-serving, satisfied to find their own peace, but seldom consider the plight of others. What's more, some staff members struggle to grow into a larger way of being. There are only seven days in a week. The Achilles' heel for many mediocre associates is falling prey to the syndrome of the daily rut.

Life is comfortable managing the same people in the same way, year by year—"us four and no more!" For growth to invade a rather mundane staff member's portfolio, there must be a radical change of heart and a new way of thinking. Change can be intimidating for the less motivated among us. Nevertheless, the real cost for growth falls squarely upon the lead pastor. To grow, from the pastor's perspective, is to learn to tolerate those who are either unlovely or obnoxiously protective of sacred cows. To grow a church is to adopt the prayer of Jabez.

"Oh, that You would bless me indeed, And enlarge my territory, that Your hand would be with me, And that You would keep me from evil,

> *Which comes first? Our hard work or God's blessing?*

that I may not cause pain" (1 Chronicles 4:10).

Certainly, church growth is a by-product of the hand of God. No one is denying that premise. We can do nothing apart from His touch. Yet a pastor must also possess an indefatigable work ethic, a crystal-clear missional focus, and an administrative capacity for strategic implementation.

Growth is elusive without an all-encompassing design plan that employs new systems and sermons, a demand for new committee assignments, and a well-marketed congregational mobilization effort. This is the stuff of giants, the veritable brass ring, if you will. Growth is not for the faint of heart.

For us, as worship leaders, church growth will make us more efficient, more industrious, and utterly more productive. Growth will cause us to reinvigorate the church calendar on a month-to-month basis. Growth provides the motivation to invent new methods and more effective training procedures. Growth will stimulate conversations around how to employ greater variety in worship, as well as greater participation from choirs, bands, and vocal ensembles. More importantly, growth will revitalize congregational participation across generational lines.

Code Orange Alert!

All in all, growth will demand a broader infrastructure in the music ministry to accommodate more diverse Christmas concerts featuring children's choirs, dance troupes, handbell ensembles, an actor's company, and ancillary personnel such as set designers, lighting specialists, painters, carpenters, storytellers, rap artists, composers, poets, and so on.

Ultimately, all people in ministry must ask, "Is a commitment to church growth worth it all?" Of course, it is because one day we'll see Jesus, and as the gospel songs remind us,

It will be worth it all

When we see Jesus.

Life's trials will seem so small

When we see Christ ...

One glimpse of His dear face,

All sorrows will erase.

So bravely run the race

'till we see Christ.[24]

Taking a City

Across the spectrum of art in a city's life, one will naturally observe classical music, opera, ballet, community choirs, jazz clubs, and college music student orchestrated presentations. Somewhere along that continuum is also a place for the best gospel choir, the best traditional sanctuary choir, and the most spirited worship team in town. In order to become the candlestick congregation, one must function on the highest level. That said, not all are called to care for an entire city. Not all can afford the expense of excellence. However, every city needs a rock-solid gospel church, which, in times of celebration or crisis, can mobilize artists to minister in the anointing of the Holy Spirit to the citywide opportunity at hand. For a list of event ideas, please see appendix 5.

These events glisten if accompanied by choral support, instrumental accompaniment, or a gifted church vocalist. Two scriptural passages clearly support this discussion.

God asks Moses, "What is in your hand?" (Exodus 4:2). This question is appropriate for the pastor who feels God's leading to care for his or her city. If the burden seems too large, then perhaps the burden is God-given. Aimee McPherson, the founder of the Foursquare denomination, built the first megachurch in America in the 1920s with the help of gypsies. The church became a city church with a large pantry, which fed hundreds daily during the Depression years, boasted a silver band of brass players numbering a hundred members, and featured dramatic Sunday evening sermons. In its prime, Angeles Temple hosted twenty-seven services weekly. Ms. McPherson was ahead of her time and is widely recognized for her creative prowess and gift of healing. She simply opened her hand.

Stories of her work are hauntingly beautiful. My favorite is that in the days before air-conditioning, one could walk the entire length of Los

---

[24] Esther Kerr Rusthol, "When We See Christ," 1941.

Angeles on a Sunday evening and never miss a word from a McPherson sermon. You see, everyone spent Sunday evening on a front porch with the windows wide open and the radio blasting for all it was worth! All across town, citizens tuned into Sister Aimee's evening service. For her church owned one of the five radio stations of the day in Los Angeles.

The men of Issachar volunteered to take up David's righteous cause, and the Bible records this apt description of this mighty band-of-brothers, "They understood the times in which they lived" (1 Chronicles 12:32). These men gleaned the discernment to fight on the right side of victory. Will you and I? Will we practice courage and understand when it is time to join the battle? Will we understand the times in which we live, mobilize accordingly, and build a worship team, a choir, mature a ministry, and take a city?

> *At worship's core, music in the church is catalytic to God's sovereign flow of grace.*

There is no doubt of music's effectiveness in sacred activity. We have delineated this concept throughout this book. Music calls us to worship. Music provides the impetus to begin a service in the mode of Psalm 100. Following an invocation and pastoral greeting, music then leads us with the skill of a seasoned tour guide toward honoring the Lord, reflecting on our trespasses, seeking forgiveness, making our petitions known, and opening ourselves up to His restorative grace and endless mercy.

> *When the stress of being blindsided mounts, He'll be your burden-bearer. When the way becomes uncertain, He deeply cares. He will direct your steps.*

What is more, the music of the church provides underscore for moments of celebration, moments of correction, and moments of a change of heart. Dr. Leonard Sweet's keen observation is not only eloquent but a fitting Christmas bow to this chapter. "In God's ears, music is the highest and purest form of prayer."

Jesus, who called you, will provide for you. You will never

> *Stay in Jesus!*

be alone. You will never be undone. So my parting blessing aptly comes from His own words. "I am the vine, you are the branches. Whoever abides in me and I in him, He it is that bears much fruit, For apart from me you can do nothing" (John 15:5).

Seeds from the Core

1. Christmas is important. Develop an annual concert for your community.
2. Support the worship team with systemic organization and devotional prowess.
3. Build a choir as soon as the church begins to grow.
4. Mature the ministry through the kinds of ingenuity that only Christ Jesus, our Lord, can provide.

EPILOGUE

As we bring our conversation to a close, I want to express my appreciation for your interest in my work. You've come to know my story and my passion for music in the church. With gratitude for your call to ministry, I want to use my epilogue to convey three concluding matters with clarity and caution. I began this book talking about my interest in the number three. Now I conclude with the same paradigm. For the number three at once reminds me that the Holy Trinity is never far from the work of our hand. Almighty God cares; Jesus, our Lord and Savior, intercedes; and the precious ministry of the Holy Spirit guides and inspires all of us who lift our voice and bend our knee.

Befittingly, I have elected to divide my concluding remarks into three sections: Contextualization, Commissioning Prayer, and Closing Activity (see appendix).

Contextualization

During the final stages of research for this book, two remarkable findings caught my attention. First, according to the landmark study by Dave and Jon Ferguson, "Each week forty-three thousand Americans are leaving the church for good." This is mind-boggling! The reasons for so precipitous a decline in church affiliation are naturally multifactorial. Still I cannot help but wonder if this congregational unrest is due, in part, to the way in which we have mismanaged worship. If my intuition is correct, it will be up to you, dear reader, to wait on the Lord for a new normal.

Alienating one generation's musical taste to prefer another's is not a biblical initiative. Rather, it is a matter of misapplied church growth philosophy. We all understand that when one is planting a new church from scratch, the song material chosen should reflect the nature of a leader's new constituency. In that regard, I am thankful for the bounty of new music, carefully composed and lyrically sound, that comes from places like Hillsong and Bethel. These collaborations are meaningful contributions to the art form you and I love.

However, before long a new church plant will age. Growth will inevitably spread beyond the target constituency to include extended family members who are excited about the changes they have seen in their sons and daughters' spirituality. When extended families respond, the new plant subtly takes on the some of the complexities of historic congregations. To effectively lead worship in a congregation of multiple generations, one has to be aware that each generation's preferences matter. Songs invoke memory. They remind us of God's rich provisions and His faithfulness throughout the years. So to entirely eliminate songs held dear in order to exclusively welcome a younger generation's preferences seems not only shortsighted but, practically speaking, deleterious. Ultimately I believe the act of blending worship, so that all in attendance can enter in and be welcomed, is an act of leadership diplomacy, practiced with world-class skill.

At worship's core, we serve to bless the Lord and minister His grace to the needs of our entire congregation. This mandate, I emphasize, is not necessarily about musical style but rather a lyrical flow of mercy—song by song—in a manner that is congruent to all who attend. Please, therefore, be a shepherd to all—the youth, the infirmed, those with young families, the empty nesters who may wonder about next steps or how to manage loneliness, the disenfranchised, the undocumented, and those without a job. All matter to God. Without a loving church family, many in our day have little with which to sustain their emotional health. For these pastoral reasons, I became a musician. When a song, either new or well-worn, can cut across the generations to land on target in the hurting human heart, all of heaven rejoices!

For me, this churchwide misunderstanding about worship could be summed up in the frustration that a recent denominational executive voiced to his cohort of ministers, saying, "I only hope this present generation lives long enough to see their form of worship completely replaced by another, as I have."

In God's timing, it has fallen on me to humbly identify a set of core values related to worship that sustained my pastoral career over the span of four decades. It is now up to you, my friend, to carry the baton of peace across your finish line.

I encourage you, therefore, to become a church musician of piety, purpose, and peace-making. It is time to restore the ailing, historic church. It is time to effectuate a new unity among all the generations who worship under your church's roof. It is time to return to what music does best, to create an atmosphere for inviting the presence of the Lord to soothe a wounded congregant by the grace of a well-conceived lyrics and provide for the lingering in His presence while the Great Physician "sets the captives free" on "the wings of a song."

You can be that guide, that vanguard! Prayer will be your key. So whatever you do, stay in Jesus! We need your inspiration and prowess now more than ever.

Commissioning Prayer

Throughout church history, God's people have encountered challenge and hardship. Many problems throughout the annals of time were far larger than ours. Consider the Crusades, the Dark Ages, and the rise of fascism, not to mention all the martyrs, famines, and failed works of the adversary.

From history, I am taken with the faith of Julian of Norwich who penned,

> *"God did not say, 'Thou shalt not be tempested, traveled or diseased.' But He did say, 'Thou shalt not be overcome!'"*

I take great comfort in those prophetic words. As you serve, bringing peace to the worship wars troubling so many congregations in this hour, the Prince of Peace will be there by your side. You are doing God's work when trying to heal a broken system of belief or countermand an untuneful fad. To further underline the need for this commissioning prayer, I have chosen a poem by the contemporary writer, Leonard Sweet, who recently shared on Facebook,

Let strife among us be unknown,

Let all contention cease;

Be God's the glory that we seek,

Be ours God's holy peace.

Let us recall that in our midst

Dwells God's begotten Son;

As members of His body joined,

We are in Christ made one.

These two quotations—linked together by our common love of Jesus's church—frame the timeless perspective, "Nothing is impossible with God" (Matthew 19:26; Luke 1:37).

God is greater than our differences and unwitting mistakes. He can turn our hearts back to the cross, healing the memories of our feckless fights. He can forgive our harsh words and bring us back together—more unified, more loving toward those who are "other than" we—more inspired to rebuild a healthy, multigenerational church, agile and strong.

With these matters clearly framed in our hearts, let us pray:

Our gracious heavenly Father, we come before You today to bless Your holy name and welcome Your presence in this prayer of commissioning. Consecrate the readers of this book with the ability to listen to the still, small voice in the middle of conflict, misunderstanding, and transition. Sanctify them as they practice contemplation, charity, and lifelong learning. Endue them with Holy Spirit courage. Enlighten them with vision and discernment, and grant them "the peace that goes beyond understanding" both in the hard times and amid the sweet victories of ministerial life. I pray in Jesus's strong name. Amen.

POSTSCRIPT

My apt editor felt that we should close with a reflection activity based upon the amalgamation of each chapter's *Seeds from the Core*. To find this exercise, please turn to appendix 1 for instructions.

APPENDIX 1

A CLOSING ACTIVITY

Now I have a challenge. I suggest you take all of my *Seeds from the Core* chapter insights and create a document for a survey. This is a document that you should complete first. In prayer and introspection, rate your church's worship needs category by category. After you have completed this assignment, ask your pastoral staff and worship team members to also take the worship survey. I have a sample document for you to work from below.

Reflect on the findings with your lead pastor first. Then with his or her consent, reflect on the findings in concentric circle of your church's leadership. The Holy Spirit will lead you in framing your future, your new normal.

What do you agree on? What are the issues that present themselves as needs for the future? What churchwide initiatives become apparent? I bless you in Jesus's strong name as you administrate this catalytic process.

The Core Issues of Worship

Rank each statement like this:

0—Most Strongly Disagree   3—Mildly Agree

1—Strongly Disagree   4—Strongly Agree

2—Disagree   5—Most Strongly Agree.

1. A theology of worship is a codified statement of what God has said about our praise and worship. _____
2. The songs of worship should reflect the taste of all the generations in the church. _____
3. Singing welcomes the presence of the Lord. _____
4. Worship is primarily about giving God the worth He truly deserves. _____
5. Worship is a participative exercise, not a concert we dutifully observe. _____
6. Our heavenly Father loves it when we sing. A song is at once an invitation, a dialogue, and a source of comfort and hope. _____
7. Our Lord Jesus is no respecter of persons. He attends to the needs of all who call on His name, in small settings or large. _____
8. The avid participation of a congregation—entering in—summons the presence of the King! _____
9. It's not the state of the art, but the state of the heart that matters most to God. _____
10. The Kierkegaard model rocked my world. It changed my focus from being the focus to being a prompter of the congregation's presentation for "the audience of one." _____
11. My prayer before planning worship has two parts. They are important to internalize. _____
12. The two revelations from my years of travel involved a congregational perspective on the worship encounter. Recall my two observations. _____

13. If we don't have a hidden life in God, our public life for God cannot bear fruit. _____

14. The relationship between a pastor and worship leader is fragile. Handle it with care. _____

15. A vibrant devotional life is essential to become the best worshipper you can possibly be. _____

16. Interpersonal skills are invaluable in the work of ministry. _____

17. Hallowed worship stimulates; hollow worship simulates. _____

18. Worship leading involves knowing how to choose songs, teach them effectively, and place them in a meaningful sequence (a flow) so the congregation can find an intimacy with Christ as they participate in corporate worship encounters that are best made in a prayerful state. _____

19. Choosing songs for worship is a multifaceted decision that is best made in a prayerful state before the Lord. _____

20. Creating a flow of worship presupposes lyrical considerations, musical sensitivity, and a keen ear to the Spirit. _____

21. Keeping all generations on the same page is a critical component of the worship leader's intercession. Unity brings the anointing. And the anointing sets the captives free. _____

22. Pastors who have experienced a troubled home life as children often relate to the church associates with frozen feelings. This matter is completely redeemable through grace. _____

23. In order to provide the worship leader the one thing necessary to be fruitful on staff, pastoral understanding and support, our leaders and worship team need to review the list of eight competencies together and evaluate where we are and how to improve. _____

24. Worship team morale is vital to keep the team unified, prayerful, and pleasant. _____

25. The battle behind the scenes rages, but "Greater is He that is within us than he that is in the world" (1 John 4:4). _____

26. Worship leaders have to develop a multifactorial skill set. They must be excellent musicians, competent administrators, and

clear-headed public speakers, capable of bringing a cogent word from the Lord to the rehearsal. _____

27. Devotions edify the workers and remind us just how able the Lord is. _____

28. From the Old Testament, three songs helped the people of Israel dominate their environment when they needed help. _____

29. The song of creativity is especially meaningful if worship leaders can apply its merit by faith. _____

30. Devotions matter. Properly communicated, they motivate spiritual commitment and build faith to minister to the people in song. _____

31. The truth in 2 Kings 3 has merit in a worship team context. Please study this passage with care and concern. _____

32. "And when the musician played, the hand of God came upon Elisha." May it fall on us as well! _____

33. God's ways are higher than ours. We must seek His help. We must rely on His ingenuity, not our own. We must also stay humble, utterly dependent on His guidance. _____

34. Christmas is important. Develop an annual concert for your community. _____

35. Support the worship team with systemic organization and devotional prowess. _____

36. Build a choir as soon as the church begins to grow. _____

37. Mature the ministry through the kinds of ingenuity that only Christ can provide. Stay in Jesus. _____

Rank order for yourself the statements so you have the top seven most important.

In your group of leaders or the worship team, add up the totals for each statement and identify the top seven priority statements for the whole group. Share that information, and then discuss how to bring more unity and agreement among the group. What issues must be addressed immediately for improvement or inclusion in the worship ministry of the church?

APPENDIX 2

A COMPILATION OF REHEARSAL REWARD SUGGESTIONS

- Begin and end on time by valuing the sacrifice the team makes to attend.
- Be extraordinarily prepared by never wasting the time of the volunteers by speaking in vague generalities or with unnecessary verbosity.
- Thoroughly plan for each minute of the rehearsal; then over plan for an extra fifteen minutes in case something you think will work falls flat.
- Remember key events in your constituency's lives like birthdays, anniversaries, promotions, graduations, the birth of a child, or the death of a loved one.
- Be transparent with your personal struggles or mountaintop experiences.
- Start each rehearsal differently! Employ humor one week and biblical promises another; show a video unexpectedly, vocalize, kneel for Holy Communion, interview a member, or invite a staff colleague to suddenly appear to bless the team.
- Share "the love" by making your team feel how special they are to you, the community, and most importantly, the Master.

- Bring refreshments occasionally.
- Take a trip together.
- Plan a picnic.
- Do something noble in the community like supporting another outreach, participating in a prayer walk, or running together in a marathon.
- Stand at the door and shake everyone's hand; end the rehearsal with hugs at the doorway (especially after a grueling rehearsal).
- Serve Holy Communion in times of consecration or hardship.

APPENDIX 3

A COLLECTION OF DEVOTIONAL TOPICS

- Being Faithful: Implications and Applications
- Counting the Cost of Christian Service
- Maintaining a Positive Attitude
- Living a Life of Gratitude
- Treating Fellow Members with Respect and Dignity
- Understanding Your Value; Finding Your Role
- Managing the Storms of Life
- Grasping Conflict Resolution
- Guarding the Tongue
- Understanding Decorum: Stage Presence and Humility
- Learning How to Effectively Lead a Congregation in Worship
- Developing a Personal Walk with Jesus
- Being Spirit-Filled and Spirit-Formed
- Accepting a Call to Intercede with Understanding
- Managing Pressure, Stress, and Busyness,
- When Answers Aren't Enough—Walking through a Lengthy Test of Fiery Temptation

APPENDIX 4

A LIST OF PROGRAM ENHANCEMENTS

- Program around a theme.
- Program around a composer's contribution to the art form or feature another time period in Christmas music history.
- Program a concert's first half with the worship team leading secular carols and Christmas standards while having the second half led by the choir and featuring five songs that tell the Christmas story—complete with narrator, soloists, and a live nativity scene.
- Conclude with an altar call built around a touching altar song.
- Plan for the presentation to be presented multiple times.
- Organize a blitz of advertising. Focus though on the all-important word-of-mouth feature—an "each one, bring one" sort of campaign.
- Build enthusiasm for two months prior to the event.
- Add corporate sponsorship.
- Hire an orchestra!

APPENDIX 5

A DIGEST OF EVENT IDEAS

- A mayor's prayer breakfast
- A citywide evangelistic effort with a notable evangelist presiding
- A citywide tragedy with prayer vigils, community marches, and ecumenical funeral services
- A commencement celebration for high school, college, or university
- A Christmas concert in the symphony hall
- A televised holiday special airing on local channels or cable outlets
- A marriage ceremony of a prominent politician or philanthropist
- A political rally in an election year
- A citywide anniversary
- A national holiday concert, picnic, or parade
- A citywide pastor's convocation, prayer initiative, or a Christmas Eve gathering
- A sudden ministry opportunity after a hurricane, earthquake, or man-made disaster

Photo Credit: Michael McDonald

ABOUT THE AUTHOR

Tom McDonald knew when he was five years old that his future would be a musical one. His parents lovingly provided a piano and top-notch instruction. He began to accompany the church choir at thirteen and began to conduct that choir at age nineteen. From that inauspicious start, those twenty voices grew to two hundred, and the Trinity Choir developed a citywide ministry which ultimately led to performances in the prestigious Joseph Meyerhoff Symphony Hall. During those twenty years of service, Dr. McDonald earned degrees in music education, with an emphasis in piano and choral conducting, as well as a PhD in church music administration.

He and his family moved to Los Angeles in 1994 to serve the ministry of Jack W. Hayford and The Church On The Way. The next fifteen years were divided into two parts, and he spent five years as a denominational leader in between. Following that experience, he received a call back to his LA roots and considered that opportunity one of the most extraordinary events of his pastoral life. It is one thing to serve a growing congregation, but to be invited back to serve a second time was an unexpected and heartwarming compliment. During his service in both long-term church settings, McDonald also taught music and worship studies in seminaries and Bible colleges. He completed forty years of service in 2014.

Soon thereafter, as a surprise second act, he accepted a post as choral director at Roosevelt High School in downtown LA. This at-risk institution is essentially populated by Latino students for whom many are bilingual. Most qualify for Title I support. In this new mission field, Tom continues to serve, to love those around him and press for musical excellence. Recently one of his students, in halting English, said, "Dr. McDonald, I have place for you in my heart!"

Contact information: tmcdonaldmusic@gmail.com

Printed in the United States
By Bookmasters